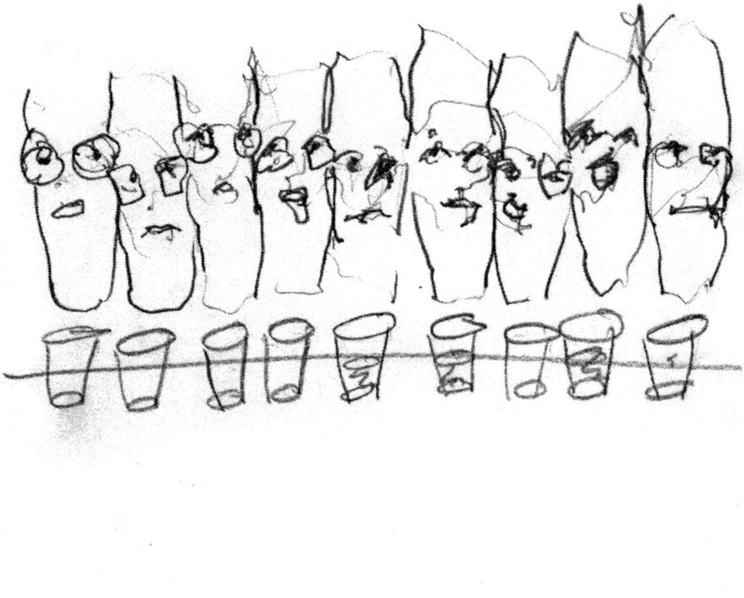

PAUL EWEN

London Pub Reviews

Illustrated by David Le Fleming

shoes with rockets

First published in Great Britain by
Shoes With Rockets, London 2007

London Pub Reviews is a work of fiction

ISBN 978-0-9555218-0-5

Cover design by Roger Kennedy
Photography by Mejor Singh
Typeset and illustrations by David Le Fleming
www.spip.co.nz

Printed and bound in Great Britain by Kall Kwik Centrepoint

www.londonpubreviews.co.uk

For my parents.

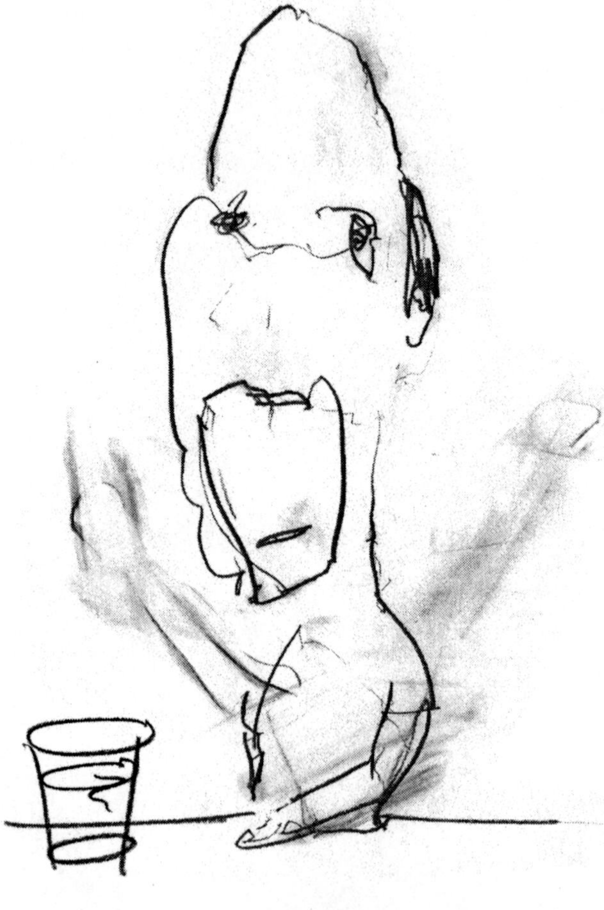

Contents

...although the pub is very much part of English culture, it also has its own 'social micro-climate'. Like all drinking places, it is in some respects a 'liminal' zone, an equivocal, marginal, borderline state, in which one finds a degree of 'cultural remission' – a structured, temporary relaxation or suspension of normal social controls (also known as 'legitimised deviance'...)

Watching the English: The Hidden Rules of English Behaviour
by Kate Fox

Introduction

This book is out of date. Sorry about that.

It's my first book as well. My first book, and it's out of date before it's even gone to the printers.

Well, I should tell you, I'm angry. I'm blimmin' angry because it wasn't even my fault. It was the developers' fault. Those blimmin' property developers...

London's back-street locals are becoming an endangered species as developers cash in on the capital's soaring prices. Latest to go are two well-known Chelsea watering holes: the Surprise in Christchurch Terrace, until recently a Good Beer Guide Regular, and the Australian in Milner Terrace... Both have been taken over by property developers, and community campaigners in SW3 are becoming alarmed at the continual erosion of the district's pubs...

Nationally, CAMRA's Pub Watch Survey finds that 26 pubs, perhaps more, are closing every month. In London, pubs are going down like ninepins as developers turn them into flats or restaurateurs seize on them as convenient shells for new ventures.

CAMRA's Greater London Regional Director Steve Williams is concerned that the loss of pubs to developers in the capital is accelerating.

He said: "The pub closure situation in London, both city and suburban, is serious. We are losing pubs to the developers at a faster rate than ever before.

We must champion the London pub, encouraging folks to use their local and emphasising that they will lose it otherwise."

- CAMRA's What's Brewing newspaper, November 2006

You see what they've done? The developers? They've only gone and closed down the Surprise in Chelsea pub, the scoundrels. They've only rendered pages 40-42 of my book completely useless. Thanks for nothing, you swine!

UNBELIEVABLE.

It's a real shame, that. But I guess we can only hope that the enclosed review of the Surprise in Chelsea will go some way towards preserving what was once a fine and decent neighbourhood pub. Not a swanky apartment filled with silly wardrobes and washing machines.

Regrettably, a few of the other pubs in this book have also changed since these reviews were first crafted, but not quite to the same extent. Not yet. Furnishings, for instance, have been moved around, or removed entirely. Dividing walls have been taken out. Fine ales in certain places, are no longer on tap. [In some cases fine ales may have never been on tap; I don't always remember, some of my notes were a bit scrunched.]

Let's hope at least that good common sense will prevail, and the true character of the London pub will remain intact. Because in this mad old world of ours, it's reassuring to know that there are still some special places where we can all go to escape from reality for a while...

March 2007

[CAMRA is actively involved in preserving London pubs. If you would like to help or find out more, please visit: www.camra.org.uk]

Central

Albert

52 Victoria Street SW1H ONP
Nearest tube – St James Park

It has been said that every Prime Minister who has ever served in Britain has been served in the Albert pub, Westminster, and as I stood outside admiring its impressive façade, I hoped that I too would soon be served inside.

Pressing forth through the main front doors, I found myself within a small enclosed entranceway, little more in size than a large telephone box. A further set of doors offered passage into the main bar itself, but as I moved towards these I suddenly felt my legs go rigid, and my arms were forced down at their sides. I appeared to be having some sort of strange turn, and as my head began to jerk violently and my body convulsed, I felt my eyelids flickering like Venetian blinds that are swiftly opened and closed with the aid of two long white cords. My legs crumpled slightly and I stumbled noisily around, bouncing off each of the four constricting walls like a fish in a shoebox.

Eventually, the whites of my eyes were replaced with normal pupils resembling oyster pearls, and I began to regain an element of control over my convulsing bodily tissues. Sweating like a shower door, I hesitantly splayed my open wet palms against the second set of glass doors and proceeded warily into the pub itself.

Upon entering the grand interior of the Albert, I quickly ascertained that everyone inside was staring at me as if I was some sort of super-freak character. A swift glance around helped me understand why. Very old illustrations were framed and mounted on the walls. An antiquarian timepiece was moulded into the woodwork above the bar, frozen in some yester hour. The windows were ornately etched with white frosted designs, and I noticed a couple of finely carved wooden booth style dividers, also with etched hand-cut glass panes. Old gas light fittings were displayed about the place, and even the ashtrays were ornately patterned and from another era entirely. In comparison, my modern hairstyle that carefully elaborated into fashionable sideburns must have appeared state-of-the-art to say the least. The bewildered stares from the gathered assembly simply reinforced what my own observations betrayed. I had journeyed back in time. Of course! It was no wonder I had become the centre of attention! I clearly looked like some sort of Tron figure to these simple salt-of-the-earths.

Tasselled ropes held back museum-piece curtains as I raised my arms in front of me as a sign of peace and open trust before announcing to the assembled crowd: "HELLO! I AM FROM THE FUTURE! I MEAN YOU NO HARM!" The patrons looked naturally apprehensive, so I attempted to calm their fears by passing around my Swatch watch and offering forth my mobile phone buttons to push.

"I AM FROM THE YEAR 2006! IN 1969 THE UNITED STATES OF AMERICA WILL PUT A MAN ON THE MOON!" Silence followed. Desperate to convince this sceptical assortment of non-believers that I was no charlatan, I continued: "TONY BLAIR IS THE CURRENT PRIME MINISTER OF THE UNITED KINGDOM." Sideward glances. "THE COACHING INN ROOMS OF MY DAY AND AGE OFFER

PAY-PER-VIEW HARDCORE SEX!"

The tense scene remained, and so I laughed, pointing at one particular gentleman, telling him that his sense of dress and style was from the old ways. It was about then that things began to turn ugly. The young gentleman in question, together with his equally incensed, solidly built fellows, marched me off in a vice-like grip, my fashionable trainers barely brushing the flowery old-fashioned carpet. I looked around in vain for assistance, instead catching a glimpse of a very old, flashing-light electronic gaming machine that stood against the far wall.

I was ejected from a bygone era through the two sets of entrance doors before being roughly deposited onto the modern tarmacked pavement outside. Brushing myself off, I hoped the Victorians I had encountered inside the Albert pub would put my Swatch and mobile phone to good use in better understanding the sophisticated ways of the 21st century.

Blackbird

209 Earl's Court Road SW5 9AN
Nearest tube – Earl's Court

It is often difficult to find a good pub near a train station. This, I think, may be because the patrons of such establishments are less interested in real ales and good service, and more keen on bursting through the doors with an unrelenting desire to urinate.

Unlike these transient types, I decided I would make the most of my time at the Blackbird, a pub situated in handy proximity to Earl's Court Station, and after requesting an ale as I passed the bar, running, I returned for my drink and calmly made my way towards a vacant table near the front.

Fortunate to be seated at the much-coveted central booth, I replenished my body with liquid and began my appreciation of the surroundings. On the partition opposite me was a beautifully framed black mirror, upon which the words BEERS PIES were ornately etched in gold-trimmed type. A green leather headrest beneath this appeared to have been scratched by a frisky, fully-grown cougar, and I hoped the publican had given the cheeky thing a firm telling off before lightly smacking its golden fur with a rolled up weekend newspaper. To my right, a frequent procession of people walked briskly past on the pedestrian thoroughfare, exposing the icy air with the exhalation of breath that their gait demanded. Of these, the occasional person would catch my eye and when they did, my face would assume an expression of extreme pain, and I would slowly mouth the words "BEERS PIES," before quickly looking away.

There seemed to be a lot of aeroplanes passing the outside of the pub also, by which I mean they weren't driving down Earl's Court Road but flying in the air. Sucking the black lid of my Nikko Finepoint 99-L pen, I nodded thoughtfully as I wrote: THE PLANE IT FLIES...PAST THE BEERS PIES.

I liked my table. It was oval and wooden and a lot of the varnish had started to come off, which was reassuring. It was reassuring because it spoke volumes about proper old-fashioned pub values and the fact that true tavern tables aren't bought over the weekend and assembled via bullet-pointed black and white assembly guides. The floor was great also. I appreciate versatility in pub flooring and I found myself spoilt for choice at the Blackbird. The front of the bar, you see, boasts sturdy wooden floorboards, while the space around the serving area bares smart black and white tiles. If you step on the cracks of these tiles or boards you'll turn into a worm and that, I believe, is actually why the pub is called the Blackbird. Adding to the floor diversity is some good old-fashioned pub carpet in the rear of the premises, suitable for the softly padding furry paws of the resident pub cougar.

The general public continued walking past the exterior of the Blackbird pub, and I noticed couples with their kids, and the kids could see me drinking liquor, but they were too young to come inside and too young to drink liquor, and it looked cold outside and I was warm as toast inside next to the radiator. A framed picture of some animals and a windmill is on the wall of the Blackbird beside the windows, and it's a picture that kids would enjoy and so I waved madly to the little ones passing by outside, pointing urgently towards the picture featuring the animals and the windmill, and when they looked at me with incomprehension, I simply helped myself to another drink of fine ale. Between large sips, I managed to write a note in bold letters upon a page in my diary, and when I'd finished, I tore it out and flashed it up at the window every time I saw some cold looking children pass by. The note read: HA, HA KIDS, YOU LOSE!

I decided to think of other notes I could write from my cosy window seat. For instance, when an aeroplane flew past, I produced a sign for the passengers who were seated on the right hand side of the craft. It read: WELCOME TO LONDON, HOME OF GREAT PUBS LIKE THIS ONE! And then for the customers coming out of the book store across the road, my notebook page sign said: READ THIS! I started placing orders at the bar via signs that I would write and wave frantically about. I also engaged with other patrons using pages of my notebook that read, NICE HAT! and ENJOYING YOUR TASTY BEVERAGE?

After I'd been doing this for about two hours, a few people wrote some notes of their own in response. One rather surly young woman wrote: GROW UP! And then a large unshaven man scrawled: PISS OFF YOU ANNOYING LITTLE PRICK!! Glad to engage in some good-natured banter, I produced a fresh sheet of paper and replied to the gent with the words: HOPE YOU TURN INTO A WORM! Well, that was about the end of the sign game as far as this particular man was concerned, and as he stormed over without so much as a glance at his big clumsy feet, I tried to write: HEY GOOD FRIEND, MIND THOSE CRACKS! But I think I only managed to write: HEY G

Bradley's

42-44 Hanway Street W1T 1UT
Nearest tube – Tottenham Court Road

The perfect time to come to Bradley's Spanish Bar is during the day, when people who talk out of their mouths and fill space with their bodies are for the most part confined to buildings where they work to earn money for pretty things.

It was 11:02am when I walked down the stairs to the basement level bar, and I held my arms aloft, scarcely containing my jubilation in the knowledge that I was their very first customer of the day. The polite and friendly barman had been cleaning and scrubbing down the serving area, and he looked up in surprise as I dramatically burst through an imaginary first place ribbon punching my fists in the air. My trophy came in the form of a pint glass full of ale, and I was happy in the knowledge that when my winning term was served out, this glass would be carefully washed and re-presented to future first place stars such as me. I placed my prize in pride of place upon an orange rectangular tabletop, and as I ran my hand along its rounded corners, I felt an urge to seize it and raise it above my ears.

A set of lower steps lead down from the Gents where they elegantly cascaded into the main bar, and smart handrails rested on either side, as if navigating patrons down into the soothing cool waters of a swimming pool. Two small enclaves to my right appeared most cosy and secluded, each dimly lit by round wall lights that one would normally encounter upon the submerged tile walls of a modern sunken pool... What in the blazes! Bradley's downstairs Spanish bar quite clearly resembled some kind of undeveloped swim-up pool bar! There was no mistake.

I let the gravity of this revelation soak in for a few seconds, like the first gentle waves that lap upon polyester swimming trunks, before I walked, as if in flippers, towards the bar for another ale. The wall-mounted jukebox was playing a catchy old-fashioned tune when I suddenly inhaled deeply, and began to rely upon my limited reserves of oxygen. My thoughts drifted at this time like dead, water-logged insects, and I began to think how the upstairs bar area could be converted into changing rooms with showers and towels. Diving or jumping off the serving counter would, of course, not be tolerated, and strictly no passing the cool liquid bar refreshments straight back into the pool water via ones' urinary tracts.

My mind wandered further towards thoughts of the whole gastro-pub experience that seemed to be gripping London. I attempted to snort with mild distain without exhaling. Why this infatuation with stripped back floorboards and exposed kitchens when we the customers could be exposing ourselves? WOBBLE YOUR LUMPY, PASTY, FAT-RIDDEN BELLIES AND REJOICE!

Other people had begun to arrive as I sat down gasping with reddened eyes and ghostly harrowed cheeks, and I watched them accept their second and third place trophies respectively, imagining warm water caressing the soft cushioning of my upholstered burgundy bench seat. Finishing my new pint in record-breaking time, I strode across to the steps and up towards the alluring toilet freshener scent that was permeating from the Gents.

Inside, I quickly unravelled reels and reels of toilet paper and set about stuffing the bunched up tissue tightly down into the brown shell-shaped washbasin. One of the taps had a head like a moose, and I turned it and its more conventional companion as far around as they would go, releasing forth a gushing of water upon the tightly compressed toilet paper dam. Another male patron was sharing the somewhat cramped Gentlemen's quarters and he looked rather quizzically at the blocked basin and rising water. After catching his eye and winking, I proceeded to punch him in the shoulder, but not too hard, and he decided against washing his hands and hastily hurried out the door. Only when I was satisfied that the rim of the basin had been breached and that water was splashing onto the floor, did I then make my own way out of the toilets and back down to my burgundy bench seat.

It was with a slight trepidation that I awaited the first trickle to escape beneath the door and find its way down the cascading pool steps. Sure enough, the first glimpse of blocked basin water wasn't long in appearing and I started removing my shoes and socks in readiness for the dipping my toes would soon be savouring in Bradley's all new pool bar. But when the barman noticed the gentle stream splish-splashing down the concrete stairs, he appeared strangely annoyed, using expletives freely, and the gent I had encountered within the Gents pointed towards me with a clearly unclean finger. Giving me a hard stare, the barman mounted the soaking steps, storming through the old wooden door towards the river's source, and a gulp began to form in my throat like a solitary bubble rising from the lowest depths of an Olympic sized swimming pool. Emerging shortly after, the young keeper of the bar proceeded to wipe his damp hands on his trousers, and the strong start I had made to the bar transformation project soon dribbled to a halt. When I began explaining to him that his work place was actually a swimming pool, he stepped closer towards me in his squelching shoes, like a lifeguard about to quash the actions of a pool bully who has been disturbing well-intentioned bathers.

As I was forcibly marched up the stairs, I imagined I was heading toward the top diving board, upon which I would gracefully leap in twisting spirals, causing barely a ripple as I made my elegant plunge into the depths of Bradley's basement bar.

Champion

12-13 Wells Street W1T 3PA
Nearest tube – Oxford Circus

The most pleasant barmaid in the Champion regarded me queerly, no doubt astounded that she could observe my arteries and intestinal workings in operation. Let me explain.

I had been scuffing my shoes along the back roads of Fitzrovia, waving out to passing red postal trucks, when I happened upon the great corner pub that is the Champion. Inside I found much character, jovial patrons and a truly winning atmosphere. The upstairs bar was packed with dining customers and extra seating, but it was the downstairs area that really made the Champion the institution it was and is. Large white and brown square tiles lined the floor around the bar, and seating was comprised of chocolate brown leather benches and many comfortable bar stools. There was a special little darts alley, and a brown tombstone shaped sign behind the bar read: PLEASE KEEP CLEAR FOR GLASS COLLECTION. However, the real highlights of this great boozer were the beautiful stained glass windows featuring images of genuine British champions.

David Livingstone, the intrepid explorer, was pictured carrying a rifle over his shoulder, cane in hand, and his sideburns looked uncannily like the floor mats just inside the doors. William Renshaw was the winner of seven singles and seven doubles tennis cups. With his brother he made lawn tennis into a sport and apparently he was fond of wearing brown slippers. I raised my glass to David, William, and to all the other great British champions preserved in glass around the bar, and I was surprised to find myself getting misty eyed at their accomplishments. But as I held aloft my cold beer, I was even more surprised to notice that my hand was actually misting up also. Wiping a clean circle of condensation from my forearm, I looked right through it to see my foot. I looked right through my foot and saw a brown tile. My entire body had turned to glass! I laughed out loud, but it wasn't my normal laugh. It was like the noise you make when you run a wet finger around the rim of a glass, and I guess it was the culmination of my saliva and my new glass larynx. My drinking vessel and the ashtray on my table suddenly seemed like brothers to me, and I gazed around the front of the bar at the established champions that welcomed me from their glass walls.

There wasn't a spare window space ready for me, so I knew in the meantime I would have to tread very carefully in my clearly fragile body. I walked with precise and calculated steps towards the bar, attracting the puzzled stares of others who were no doubt drawn by the sound of my feet clinking on the tiles like a champagne flute being flicked. I was careful not to chip my toes on the golden tubular footrest that ran around the bottom of the serving area, and I sought out a clean bar towel and set about polishing myself until I gleamed like a royal wedding souvenir goblet. My new falsetto voice sounded like a choirboy's when I ordered another drink, and the barmaid stared perhaps too long at my quivering heart that pumped blood around my delicate glass interior.

After carefully making my way back to my seat, I made a start on my drink and amused myself for a while by watching it run down into my see-through stomach and slosh around. This was particularly funny when I twisted my hips a bit. I could have amused myself for hours with this, but looking around at the various glass champions that lined the windows, I felt an impatient longing to take my rightful place amongst them. So I stood on one of the dark chocolate leather bench seats and gently leaned against the cocoa wall, assuming a pose with raised drink in my right hand, chin atop the shiny knuckles of my left. You could say I was debonair, and perhaps even rather dashing. "I'M SHY REALLY," I said with a bashful smile to the approaching barmaid, but my smile was somewhat lost on her, perhaps behind her apron, and she demanded that I get my filthy bowling shoes off the bar seating. I protested of course, resisting her outstretched hand, instead resuming a new pose that revolved around fingering a feathery quill.

Unfortunately, I kind of lost my balance at this point, and I fell sideways off the bench seat onto a small round bar table with black wrought iron legs. The subsequent noise sounded like a stolen truck being driven through a department store window, and I instantly smashed into one hundred thousand shards all across the white and brown square tiles. However, the quick thinking and attentive staff soon had me swept up into a plastic tray, and after pouring me into a newspaper and folding this into a rough ball, I was added to the cigarette butts and empty peanut packets in the large rubbish bin out back.

Coach & Horses

29 Greek Street W1V 5LL
Nearest tube – Leicester Square/Tottenham Court Road

The Coach & Horses is a modest, yet monumental pub landmark in Soho, made famous by a bad-mannered publican, a foul-mouthed newspaper columnist, and some legendary £1 sandwiches.

I arrived soon after opening time on a drizzly weekday morning, and I quickly made my way towards the servery, where I stood upon a footrest that resembled an indented strip of toothpaste. A drink list behind the bar contained individual gold letters like a hotel foyer sign, welcoming me as a visiting conference delegate, while a more basic laminated sign advertising Sandwiches £1 All Day was taped beneath the lift-up servery top. On a wall to the left of the bar, a poster mentioned: TERRORISM, BOMBS, BE ALERT. When the barmaid gave me my change, I pointed to this poster, making explosive sounds and laughing.

Making myself comfortable behind a black squared table that backed onto Greek Street, I noted that the barstools and chairs were varying lipstick shades of red in their leather seating, describing my own upholstered chair as CHIMNEY POT LUSCIOUS. A ceiling that appeared to be made out of a honey substance merged into the custard-like upper walls, and these bore framed comic strip illustrations that brought to life the antics of various characters from the establishment's much lauded past.

Cheese, tomato and lettuce were layered between two slices of brown bread and served upon a white plate with a green rim. My £1 also provided for a neatly folded paper napkin, a stainless steel knife engraved with the words, Sheldon Cutlery Stainless Steel, and a jar of original pickle. Of course, knowing such a soggy, paste-like congealment of bread and cheese would only cling in a mollusc-like way to my gums and teeth, I decided not to eat my sandwich, and began instead to study the base of my plate.

Sampsonite Churchill England Super Vitrified 89 was inscribed upon its curved bottom, and as I held it aloft like a sacrificial lamb, crumbs ran off its vertically leaning porcelain slope like tiny alpine ski jumpers made of bread, each morsel leaping record distances before landing safely in the soft folds of my grey, school-like jumper.

I was picking out the better padded of these competitors and swallowing them whole, when a suspicious package was violently jammed through a slot in the unvarnished side door to Greek Street. Landing with a thump on the carpet, the parcel appeared to be comprised of various loose items that were held together by two criss-crossing red rubber bands, both stretched tightly across a plain white envelope to make it resemble a St. George's flag. I watched as a sinister looking silhouette slipped away along Greek Street behind the guise of the blurred, frosted windows of the bar and a thick red jacket. The bar staff were busy keeping patrons' glasses well-filled, and having briefly visited the Gents, I knew they had more work ahead of them trying to get that place cleaned up. I would have to go it alone, so I picked up the stainless steel knife that Sheldon Cutlery had produced for the slicing of soft bread.

"CUT THE RED WIRE!" The other patrons glanced across at me as if somehow alarmed, and realising I had shouted my thought process aloud,

I gestured softly with my hands in a yoga-like movement, as if I were pressing a terrorist's head beneath warm soapy bath water. It was crucial that I didn't spark a thunderous stampeding panic amongst the civilians. So I whistled. I think I whistled something by Kool & the Gang. Then I crept stealthily across the red flowery carpet like a lizard in human clothing and shoes.

There was no ticking. My ear was cocked for telling signals or beeps, but despite the lack of piped music in the bar and the fact that the other customers had stopped talking to observe me, I could still detect no audible sensor or timer device. The different envelopes appeared to be addressed to the landlord of the Coach & Horses, and producing the knife, I began carefully slicing through the first red rubber band that was tightly fastened around the white A4 envelope. Despite my cautious approach however, I was caught off guard when it suddenly snapped without warning, causing me to shriek and flap my arms about like a knife-wielding albatross chick. Blind with fear, I began to stab the entire package in an uncontrollable sewing machine-like fashion. Shreds of ripped paper began accumulating across the carpet until I eventually ceased my thrusting, searing motion, gasping. Satisfied that no explosive devices were forthcoming, and finding no Anthrax powder distributed upon the red carpet fibres, I cautiously began a slow retreat back to my table in order to finish the remainder of my drink and to gently mop up the odd stray breadcrumb with a moistened fingertip.

A person with a Metropolitan Police insignia emblazoned on their vest began approaching me after conversing with the bar staff, and so I began to hastily arrange a pretty dove shape out of my unused paper napkin. But I had only folded the beginnings of a tissue beak when the constable grabbed my shoulder, causing my face to contort into an amusing, illustrated cartoon caricature.

French House

49 Dean Street W1D 5BG
Nearest tube – Leicester Square

A London pub that doesn't sell pints of beer might sound like some flight of fancy, but if you open your mind to a different drinking culture entirely, then a whole new world can be found awaiting at the French House pub in Soho.

At 12:04pm on a pleasant Friday morning, I stood outside on the concrete block pavement and, cupping my hands around my face like wrinkled racehorse blinkers, I peered in through the white-frosted windows. This was to be my first glimpse of an exotic, foreign drinking house.

Upon entering the premises themselves, I was immediately taken by the very small surroundings, cluttered as they were by all manner of photographs, paintings and illustrations. Enquiring as to the costs of hiring an audio guide, in English, in order to aid my studied browsing of the artworks upon the walls, the barman lifted his hands before him in an easily understandable gesture of incomprehension. I laughed, only too aware of the cultural divide that separated us. But this chasm deepened soon after when he informed me that the pub only served ale in half-pint glasses. WHAT THE...? Obviously familiar with the naïve likes of me, he slowly repeated this charming local tradition, and shaking my head, I dispensed with some coinage of his fair currency, and left the servery with 300mls of ale.

My early arrival had been rewarded however, with a prime corner bench seat in a cul-de-sac to the rear of the bar, and I made claim to this position by arranging the contents of my pockets in neat, horizontal piles across the table, like the contents of a small nation's time capsule. The half pint of ale I had purchased was, of course, now empty, and as the barman again filled my small glass, he resembled a petrol station attendant refuelling a vehicle that has just left the station, driven once around the block, and immediately returned with an empty tank.

Despite the clink of glasses, and coins being fingered within the pockets of the cash register tray, the only noise of note in the bar was the constant hum from a vent in the wall above my seat. Ghosts speak through radio static, and I was listening out for them in the fan when my mobile phone suddenly rang loudly with its distinctive 'Easy Lover' ring-tone, a track first brought to life in 1984 by English musician Phil Collins and his American counterpart, Phil Bailey. I let it ring for sometime, worried at first that I would have to pay overseas charges if I answered, but just then the barman stuck his head around my back corner of the bar and loudly exclaimed, "NO MOBILE PHONES IN THE BAR! THANK YOU!" An accusing silence sounded like a pane of glass that had been kicked in by a yellow boot roller skate. No mobile phones? What queer custom was this?

Back at the bar, having just broken the rules and traditions of the local ways, I attempted to play my appeasement card by requesting a bottle of fine French wine and "uno" glass. The barman smiled slightly, as if in pain, and he fetched a bottle and set about uncorking it. Once seated again, I began writing myself a postcard on a piece of scrap paper:

DEAR PAUL,
HELLO! I'M AT THE FRENCH HOUSE PUB IN SOHO. DRINKING FRENCH WINE! HERE'S TO YOU! AM FULLY ABSORBED IN THE CULTURE HAVING SPOKEN OFTEN TO A LOCAL MAN WHO KNOWS ME WELL. MY TABLE IS CLEAN. THEY ONLY SERVE HALF PINTS! MOBILES ARE BARRED! AND THEY DON'T OPEN UNTIL MIDDAY! HOW ARE THINGS SOUTH OF THE RIVER? FOR GOD'S SAKE, DON'T OPEN THE DOOR FOR ANYONE AND NEVER ANSWER THE PHONE! ALL THE BEST! PAUL.

Just then, the barman placed a simple glass bowl before me, filled with fresh olives. Smiling, he said: "ENJOY!" I was taken aback. What a kind and generous act! He disappeared again, and deeply moved, I felt tears begin welling in my eyes. I was dabbing at these when a sharp voice nearby said: "GROW UP YOU BIG CRY-BABY." I glanced around, fearing that it was the voice of a French ghost speaking through the soft baritone hum of the extractor fan. "YOU STUPID TOURIST JERK WATER." The words seemed to come from beneath my very nose, and as I looked down, I saw the open end of an olive move to perfectly form the shape of the word "PRICK." More olives began piping up with insults out of fish-like mouths. It was extraordinary! Talking olives! In perfect English! The next thing I knew, a chorus of olives had begun loudly humming the 'Easy Lover' tune of my mobile phone ring-tone, and the barman looked quite angry when he suddenly appeared again, making it clear in no uncertain terms that mobile phones were not welcome in the French House.

I had an olive squeezed into each eye socket when I returned to the bar, because they'd been very insistent in their demands to see the wine list. But the barman showed me the door instead, and I wish I'd left some more room on my postcard to mention the really early closing hours.

Jeremy Bentham

31 University Street WC1E 6JL
Nearest tube – Warren Street

While the physical remains of Jeremy Bentham are carefully housed in University College London, his good name is preserved in this delightful corner pub nearby. Five fine ales are well kept on the premises also, and you can find details of these on a blackboard behind the bar.

After settling myself upon a bench seat just inside the door, I placed my five pints of ale on what was distinguished as the number '4' table via its small round corner plaque. The clientele appeared amenable, and I began discreetly eavesdropping on their conversations, quickly gauging that my fellow patrons included students and small groups of senior academics. It appeared to be a stomping ground for higher education types, an observation that seemed verified by the many different blackboards in the ground floor bar area.

Spotted Dick and Custard had been chalked up on the SPECIALS blackboard near the staircase to the upstairs bar, and a small portable blackboard on the bar top promoted other desserts, such as Bread & Butter Pudding. Sixteen different wines were listed on yet another blackboard, and I dutifully copied down the chalk-written figures that explained the prices by the bottle or the glass. But my mind was already wandering. I was unstimulated, desperate to learn more. What was the soil temperature of the Rioja Campo Viejo Spanish red? Or the corkage wood of the Italian Pinot Grigio? I began fidgeting in frustration, doodling lurid scenes on my table top. Other patrons seemed to have lost all interest too. Many of them were speaking loudly and laughing, some unruly types were smoking openly, and I even heard one man using SWEAR WORDS. This would not do. It was time for discipline to make a healthy return to the Jeremy Bentham.

I was clutching my one remaining pint of ale when I strode purposefully across to the TODAY'S CHOICES blackboard, and after placing my glass on the mantelpiece beneath, I proceeded to wipe the entire menu off with my sleeve. Turning to face the bar, I clapped loudly for attention. Then, seizing a stump of chalk I wrote in bold capital letters: LESSON ONE.

Blank faces stared at me, and when a cheeky fellow continued talking aloud, I pointed my finger at him and shouted "HAH!" Announcing the title of my lecture as "A STUDY OF KNEE AND NOSE TISSUE FIBRES," I was met with a barrage of open scoffs and sniggers. Despite my stern tone, I realised there were clearly some problem elements that I would need to contend with. Wiping chalk dust off my ear, I pressed the upper rim of some non-existent spectacles into the base of my forehead. "HEADS SHOULDERS KNEES AND NOSE, KNEES AND NOSE," I began. Great booming laughter erupted throughout the bar, and I felt my cheeks redden and the back of my neck boil with sweat.

"SILENCE!" I screamed, throwing my pint of ale to the floor with an almighty crash. "SIT DOWN!"

A deathly quiet suddenly descended, and satisfied that a sense of order had been recaptured, I cleared my throat to continue. But my lesson was again interrupted when members of the bar staff began approaching the front of the class without permission.

Later, seated at a wooden bench seat outside the Jeremy Bentham pub, I proceeded to write FAIL, FAIL, FAIL upon the backs of random beer mats that I had grasped at the point of my sudden departure.

Nag's Head

53 Kinnerton Street SW1X 8ED
Nearest tube – Hyde Park Corner/Knightsbridge

A previous reviewer once described the Nag's Head mews pub as, "a slice of countryside just a stone's throw from Knightsbridge." The roof tiling I struck with my jagged piece of broken concrete was some distance from the Knightsbridge that I knew however, and while I don't go to a fancy gym, I do have a stronger arm than a very old woman close to death, for example.

Despite this, the pub's small and modest exterior does offer a nod towards a rural flower cart, particularly in summer. Its fronting becomes impressively decked out with a vast array of beautiful floral arrangements, which make the expensive cars outside appear like Soviet tractors or quaint, rusting farm implements. Inside, certifications from various floral and gardening groups accredit the Nag's Head for its exquisite bloom presentations, and for demonstrating that pubs needn't always smell of beer-drenched carpet, soiled trousers and burnt tyres.

The grey-haired head of the cheerful barman barely reached the height of my thigh, due to the much sunken area behind the bar, and I laughed slightly as I ordered a pint of good old-fashioned rural ale. With drink in hand, I then walked in clumsy, Wellington-laden feet towards a small round table near the front windows, inadvertently spilling some of my well-topped up pint glass onto the thirsty floor beneath.

I was suckling like a smelly little pig at the rim of my glass soon after when I suddenly heard what sounded like a large hotdog emerging from a deep-fried batter cocoon. Cocking my head around my table, I watched round-eyed as a tree began sprouting through the floor near the remnants of my spilled ale. Its lichen covered trunk ascended quickly as if spurred on by magic beans, causing me to raise my legs as the thin wooden floor area began lifting with the strength of the expanding roots beneath. Astonished, I looked around the bar at the other lunchtime patrons, attempting to share a fellow headshake of disbelief, but they all stared back at me blankly, as if chewing on hay.

When the upper branches had reached the brown plaster ceiling and continued to spread out at pace, I turned my attention to the contents of my glass. Somewhat apprehensive, I took a few hesitant sips. Finding no traces of fertiliser or liquid compost however, I thirstily gulped it down like a young Enid Blyton character in need of a quenching after digging a large open grave. After returning from the bar with another fresh pint, I decided to climb the tree and hide amongst its extensive foliage.

As a fully-grown male, full of ale and cheese, I was quick to discover that the upper branches were fairly lean, even bordering on the spindly. I cautiously positioned my feet on the questionable creaking wood, feeling slightly fearful as they began to bend substantially beneath me. Bushy tailed grey squirrels looked on as I walked tightrope style in a long descending arch, eventually finding myself grounded again at the floor of the bar. Rather than facing a giant at the top of my magic beanstalk as it were, I was instead faced with the midget-like staff who were almost hidden in the sunken serving area behind. Keeping my feet pressed upon the far end of the branch, I purchased another brim-filled pint of rural ale, the balance of my outstretched arms briefly compromised as I reached for my wallet and fingered for the appropriate change.

The publican showed no apparent interest in the tree that was now sprouting out all over the place in the middle of his bar, and after turning, I repeated my steady footsteps back along the desperately thin branch, regrettably spilling much of my glass's contents through the foliage and onto the brown fertile floor base beneath. By the time I had settled again in the upper wedge of the tree, a veritable national park of forest area had sprung up within the Nag's Head pub, weaving itself around a carefully nurtured collection of memorabilia that had in turn grown upon the pub's wood–framed walls. All was serene in my perch, and I smiled as a leaf fell gently into my ale.

Just then, a very fierce wind began to blow and I don't know where it came from because the door and windows were closed. Swaying desperately, I attempted to clasp for dear life to the moss-covered boughs, but my Wellingtons lost their footing and I toppled down onto the floor with a whump, my ale and glass scattering like pollen seeds in the wind. The publican had now doubled in size, and as I pointed to the top of the tree he shook his head and looked instead at the broken glass.

Outside, I began to sing shrilly like a starling, lightly tapping on the window with my craggy stiff beak.

Prince of Wales

150-151 Drury Lane WC2B 5TD
Nearest tube – Covent Garden

This well-established pub sits on the bottom corner of an imposing white-stone building on a street known for its theatres and tourist spots. It's a building with a long and varied history, and a plaque on the wall outside declares that the bar area has even served as a potato warehouse in times gone by. Nowadays the large square structure has pretty flower arrangements draping its many windows, and you can store potatoes in yourself when you eat them cooked with your delicious pub meal. There can be no doubting the illustrious past of the grand Prince of Wales, and if you're in the area you should most definitely drop by for a drink.

It's funny though, but I have to admit that when I first sat down at my table inside, I was actually a bit taken aback by the curtains. Goodness! I thought. They're a bit over the top for a sturdy old drinking establishment aren't they? You see, the curtains inside the Prince of Wales are all flowery and puffed up and frilly at the top. They're tied like a young girl may tie her hair in pigtails, and if you happen to have tattoos like I do, you tend to sit and rub your stubbly chin for a minute or two and ponder all those pub fights that you once heard about from someone. In fact, I even remember thinking to myself: This is not a pub; it's a bleeding doll's house.

But then that was when it clicked. Of course, that was the theme! It's supposed to be one of those antique Victorian doll's houses, but with a bar. The curtains, the plants in the window sill, the flowery seat covers and the flowery carpet design. Suddenly it all made sense. It was still as hard as the next place, but the proprietors were clearly just being a bit smarter and a bit more innovative by catching those lucrative tourist dollars while still continuing to dish out good old-fashioned booze to us rough boys. I had a belly laugh and decided that you had to admire their ingeniousness. I also decided that since I was there I should get into the theme of things as well, and I'd start by walking to the toilet like a doll and see if any of the staff picked up on the fact that I knew exactly what was going on.

Now as you may have observed yourself, when a child walks a doll along, they kind of jump it along in small hops rather than actually walking it because the doll's legs don't tend to bend much. It's actually harder than it sounds, but I'm sure if I'd had more chances to practise, I would have won favour with the bar staff and maybe got my photo on the wall or something. Anyway, I stood up from my table and hop-walked off along the raised carpeted area of the bar towards the polished floorboards and in the general direction of the toilets. I should mention also that I had a massive big smile on my face, like really big, and my eyes were really wide open, except for when I did a wink to the bar staff as I hop-walked-jumped past the bar area.

Once inside the Gents I had to double over and catch my breath somewhat, because I'll tell you what, you need to be fit if you're going to come into the Prince of Wales and do this on a regular basis. When I jumped back again, I think the staff got it, the doll walk I was doing, and appreciated it. A lot of the customers stopped what they were doing and looked at me very strangely, and I guess they were the tourists who had just arrived and still hadn't yet picked up on the theme. Once I'd sat down again, I had a drink from my pint, but like a doll would do it, without really bending my body, so I leaned way back on a tilt so I could get my mouth level with the edge of my glass. Also, because dolls can't actually drink anything, I pursed my lips so the ale just ran straight off my lips down my chin and all over my shirt, trousers and the flowery carpet. It was so funny!

I was really getting into the great theme when the bartender came over with a cloth and asked me to leave. I laughed, but he was very angry. I stood outside feeling a little disappointed and confused and my shirt and pants were all damp because it was very cold.

Princess Louise

208 High Holborn WC1V 7EP
Nearest tube – Holborn

The Princess Louise is reputed to house the finest Victorian pub interior in London, and in my opinion, its Gents' toilets alone contain more craftsmanship and character than any chain pub I could mention. Built in 1872 and immaculately refurbished in 'gin palace' style in 1891, its exquisite features have thankfully been preserved for anyone who walks in off the street and buys a drink.

I dropped by on a Saturday afternoon, choosing to reside in the carpeted front area of the bar. A small round table held my pint of ale, and my leather upholstered bench seat was the colour of spooned baby food. Behind me was a stretched entranceway to the street, and etched windows to my left offered a slightly distorted view of a boring, lesser world outside. It was from my comfortably couched vantage point that I absorbed the ornate wood and plasterwork, the decorated tiles, the intricately designed gilt mirrors and the ornately patterned red and gold ceiling. A pub truly made for a princess, and also an older man I observed who broke wind on a barstool and looked around and smiled to himself.

I was admiring the breathtaking Victorian splendour when I noticed a gambling machine alongside the opposite wall. It resembled some sort of new-fangled techno music box, and its lurid flashing lights quite simply made a fool of the pristine, Grade II listed surroundings. What's more, it was blocking the beautifully opulent mirror design behind it, which featured etched butterflies and plant-life. Quite simply, it was mocking the Princess. Shaking my head vigorously, I then observed a second gambling machine to my right, its crass circus lights flashing like an obscene man near a seesaw in a small, residential park. This was an outrage. Some scruffy young tearaways had clearly been defiling the premises, and the bar staff in their smart white shirts and black trousers had somehow overlooked the vandalism. I thought about mentioning it to them, but they looked pretty busy keeping the customers very happy, so I decided to deal with the matter myself.

I was wearing clean clothes and undergarments when I unplugged the gambling machine near the right wall, instantly killing its bright and flashing display. Shuffling it from side to side, I slowly began moving it across the floorboards towards the door, where I negotiated some rough brown carpet and small mosaic tiles until I had it outside on the rough concrete pavement. When I started moving the other machine, one of the bartenders looked at me quizzically, but I just pointed at the machine and raised my eyebrows as if to say, "THOSE CRAZY KIDS!" Winking, I continued shuffling it out the door.

Soon a handful of bar staff had joined me outside with their hands on their hips, watching as the second gambling machine joined the other on the footpath. When I saw their concerned expressions, it suddenly dawned on me that they were assuming I'd put the machines in the bar in the first place. GOOD LORD! Determined to set the record straight and to show my absolute contempt for these appalling monstrosities, I proceeded to push the first gambling machine firmly out onto the road.

No sooner had it landed on its painted glass face with a smash, than a swiftly moving bus happened by, making short work of the stupid plastic glass box and all its fancy electrical wizardry.

Gold coins ran freely down High Holborn, but not tempted by their bright, enticing glare, I instead turned my attention towards the second machine before being pinned to the ground and restrained. The Saturday afternoon crowd looked on hesitantly, and I didn't manage to finish off my pint of very fine ale, which will clearly be somewhat tepid by the time you read this.

Red Lion

1 Waverton Street W1J 5QN
Nearest tube – Green Park

In modern Mayfair, a beacon to the old ways can still be found along the narrow corner path of Waverton Street. The surrounding area was fields when the Red Lion was first placed upon the good earth, but it's possible that the farmers up and left when their local pub affixed a sign to the door which read: IT IS HOUSE POLICY THAT ALL CUSTOMERS SHOULD BE SUITABLY DRESSED. PERSONS WEARING OVERALLS OR SOILED JEANS WILL NOT BE ADMITTED.

My jeans resembled daggy rags, torn to shreds about the knees, and their pockets contained unwashed handkerchiefs and collected tufts of bellybutton fluff. Fearing immediate expulsion as I entered the bar therefore, I bent my torso forward so my hands would cover the patches of my bare lower thigh, and I half-ran to the servery in this huddled over fashion, greatly appreciating the traditionally styled carpet. Banging my head hard into the bar counter after misjudging the distance from the door, I quickly covered my error by urgently patting my well-groomed hairstyle across my forehead bruising.

The rather well-to-do clientele were befitting to the area, and conscious that I was desecrating the main bar with my tatty wardrobe and unshaven, messy face, I stealthily crept around to the room at the rear. After placing my ale upon a small wooden table, my bottom slowly descended like a helicopter onto a brown bar seat, as if it were a landing pad marked with a capital 'B'. The back bar was cosy and quaint, with antique plates and ornaments carefully mounted on raised wall shelving. A small adjoining restaurant seemed distinguished and inviting, but I decided to order from the bar menu at my table, requesting a Cottage Pie in fitting with my mid 18th century surroundings. I had no intention whatsoever of actually eating the meal of course, instead deciding to test a hypothesis that I deemed useful for the bar patrons and the greater scientific community. Based on the decorated plates on the upper shelving of the back room bar, my experiment would seek to chart the gradual growth of mould, in the same way that a wall chart measures a child's growth via pencil markings. In the case I was proposing however, the child would be a mix of gravy, grease and assorted food types, and the growth would come in the form of bacteria and toxic rot.

Rather than shovelling down the Cottage Pie therefore, I instead picked up my plate and walked across to a bench pew, before clambering up onto its curved wooden headrest. Wobbling slightly, I delicately placed my plate of pie in a vertical position on the upper shelving, balancing it against the wall between some Toby Jugs and some spotless members of the dish fraternity. Back at my table, I was watching my meal begin its descent down the dish when a helpful member of staff attired in pressed black trousers came looking for my dirty plate. Finding only gleaming cutlery and a well-pressed napkin, she looked somewhat perplexed as I politely belched and vigorously rubbed my tummy in a circular motion. Her eyes wandered briefly across my clothing, as if to search for a large concealed, disc-shaped item, while behind her, the remains of my lunch slithered grotesquely to the plate's bottom rim, resulting in a small accumulated mound of stodge upon the upper wooden shelf.

Observing the tedious formation of bacterial fungi is a process that involves months of meticulous commitment, so aware that patience would be necessary in my quest for the Nobel Prize, I stood up and stretched my legs. Just outside the narrow doorway nearby was a signed photograph of Charles Conrad Jr., a NASA astronaut who once visited the Red Lion and consumed a pint of stout in capsule form. From this, my eyes were drawn to the delightful coloured glass panels in the back bar ceiling, and I decided to head outside in search of access to the roof.

A large and sturdy vine stem was affixed to the wall to the left of the entrance door, and I soon scaled this and some ivy further up. Creeping across damp roof tiles in torn, Tarzan-like attire, I found myself looking down onto the Red Lion's back bar ceiling. After giving the thumbs up in white-gloved hands, I leapt spread-eagled into space.

The coloured ceiling glass panels gave way without a quip, and my almighty landing on the carpet made all the porcelain pieces on the shelving jump slightly. Worried that I may have begun burning to a crisp after re-entering through the Earth's atmosphere, I crawled in some pain towards a fire extinguisher that hung beside the open brick fireplace. I was lunging out with inches to spare however, when a plate slid off the upper shelf, encrusting my head with a crown of pie and porcelain pieces.

Sun Tavern

66 Long Acre WC2E 9JH
Nearest tube – Covent Garden

Try and arrive early at the Sun Tavern so you can get a chance to sit at what must surely be known as the Special Table. It's special because it is tall and round with a large golden ring that runs around its circumference, and it commands the prime drinking spot at the front of the bar by the window. All the other tables in the Sun Tavern are much lower to the ground and come in your usual sizes, shapes and materials. The Special Table, however, is quite clearly the place upon which to rest your delicious pint of ale. It's something else, the Special Table.

I first noticed it when I walked past outside and, more importantly, I noticed it wasn't occupied. Standing at the bar soon after, waiting for my drink to be poured, I couldn't help feeling that someone could walk through the door at any minute and slide up to the Special Table before me. Realizing that I was sweating and twitching and attracting strange glances from the staff and patrons, I tried to ease the tension by pulling some funny faces, as I looked around at the other features of this small cosy pub.

At the back of the bar I noticed a Wurlitzer-shaped oval archway which led to the toilets and a roped off staircase. Four large mirrors hung opposite the serving area, along with small, framed pictures on the wooden wall partitions between them. Such charming decorations, I thought, biting white knuckles. My darting eyes flicked back to the bar, but my ale was still being poured. Terrified, I looked again towards the framed pictures. How cute they were. How very cute. I squeezed out a painful smile just as the mirror reflection revealed the barmaid placing my full glass onto the bar behind me, and I turned as if in spasm, and snatched it away from the bar top before running at pace to the Special Table laughing, "HA! HA! HA! HA!"

I sat atop one of the towering green vinyl cushioned chairs and placed my bag on another, my coat on another and my handkerchief and socks on yet another, just in case anyone tried to muscle in. I had secured the Special Table and it felt great. I sat there applauding my success and raised my glass to the other patrons and to everyone walking past the window outside. The golden ring around the Special Table really was amazing to behold, and as I sat there I thought I'd try my hand at steering it. So I took hold of the polished gold rail and manoeuvred it in an anti-clockwise direction, and as the table moved slowly around, all of the street lights outside suddenly dimmed.

I didn't think much of this at first, but when I turned it back the other way, the lights all became bright again. I laughed out loud. Then I moved it back the other way again and all the parked cars outside suddenly moved backwards really quickly by themselves and the streetlights dimmed once more!

I kept turning it faster and faster and cars came whizzing back past the bar and people also, all running backwards. The hands on my watch were flying around anti-clockwise, and my pint glass started emptying and refilling itself. The fancy new building over the road disappeared into the ground and an old character building from the nineteenth century replaced it, and the cars flying backwards past the window began to look like old vintage cars and the people weren't dressed very fashionably. Meanwhile I kept turning and turning the gold rail on the Special Table and then dinosaurs started flying backwards outside and the barmaid tapped me on the shoulder and said, "I think you should leave now."

I went outside and everything had returned to normal again, but my arms really hurt.

Surprise in Chelsea

6 Christchurch Terrace SW3 4AJ
Nearest tube – Sloane Square

The Surprise resides in a nice and pretty neighbourhood, and as I made my way along the pleasant streets a couple of dogs barked sharply at me. My nerves aren't what they used to be, but I managed to smile faintly and whisper back, "Hey friends, you smell good too!"

A collection of elderly people were sitting outside under umbrellas when I arrived, and I smiled warmly at them, politely tipping my imaginary peaked cap. Inside, I gave the pleasant barman a knowing nod and directed my pint towards the red-carpeted back room to the right of the bar. In front of my chosen armchair was a little table with a large black ashtray in its centre, and on the walls were various works of art, together with their explanatory titles, sizes and prices. Although the table before me was wooden and small, the chair in which I sat was soft and huge, and it was upholstered in a flower-patterned light green.

As soon as I sat down, I felt like I was drowning. My small bottom disappeared somewhere below me, and my arms and legs started flailing around like the tentacled stems of a submerged river plant. I tried to reach for my ale, but I simply sunk further into the light green, flower-patterned upholstery, and it dawned on me that I was, perhaps, in dire danger. Fortunately, just then a very sweet older woman on her way to the Ladies heard my cries and whimpers and loud gargling noises, and she lent me a frail old arm to assist in my recovery. Well, I should tell you that I'm not a large or strong man, and in fact I'm very much neither of these things, but despite this and despite the dear old madam's best intentions, well I quite simply yanked her right off her ruby red heels and onto the waves of light green, patterned flower cushioned upholstery. She squealed in an old-fashioned way as the two of us rocked and swayed and bucked in the huge old chair, and I looked desperately across to the small table and my unattainable glass of ale.

A bony elbow struck me in the face and for a minute the rustic red walls became a blur as my saviour of sorts floundered around above me, crying and screaming and cursing. I needed to drink fluids, while my bucking, talcum-sprinkled passenger clearly needed to dispense with some. Thankfully, a second old woman then passed us on her journey towards the Ladies, and she stopped with a vein-laden hand across her mouth at the sight of us squirming about in the chair. "HELP ME!" cried my bony-elbowed dame of good intention, thrusting her hand out to this other woman who was also brimming with urine. Can you guess what happened next, pub enthusiast? Yes. This second good Samaritan was thus hoisted afloat the turbulent tides of back room upholstery, with me pinned, punctured and drowning beneath the pair of them.

With three of us now riding the perilous spring cushioned waves, there was clearly a commotion ensuing that was contrary to the Surprise in Chelsea's reserved and modest ways. Unsurprisingly, a small army of people, comprising bar staff, regular customers, and large husbands and sons, quickly emerged to find two exceptionally well-respected old women of the community being tossed and turned above a churning tide of young, small drunken man.

In retrospect, I should have sat near the front of this great pub, where the lower window-panes are stained in lovely green shades, a Bar Billiards table is nearby, and the seats are sturdy wooden chairs with tables at a sensible height. As it was, strong, hairy hands replaced the frail, bony arms of my two lovely old shipwreck companions, and I was scooped out of the cushioned waves and thrust onto the dry, safe streets of Chelsea. And when I passed the barking dogs, I had no counter to their claims of my putrid sweat, nor that of my foul, unsightly breath.

City

Bricklayer's Arms

63 Charlotte Road EC2A 3PE
Nearest tube – Old Street

Situated on a back street corner in Shoreditch, the Bricklayer's Arms is popular with a younger, more scruffy type of pub patron, who can be found sitting with their shirts untucked on chairs made from drained keg barrels.

Seating was limited on the day I visited, so I stood beside the windows opposite the serving area, my pint glass fighting for room on a ledge commandeered by a plethora of flyers, magazines and discarded newspapers. Ernest Hemingway used to write standing up, and I followed the big man's way, attempting to make notes in the dimly lit surroundings, while my thoughts drifted to a large fish I would later wrestle and nail to my wall. A coat-stand stood in solidarity alongside me, keeping hats and jackets from the blackened floorboards, and my jottings were illuminated by red lamps by the window that reminded me of small pumpkins with claws. Behind the long and welcoming bar was a particularly complex line-up of pouring taps, including centrally placed ale-pulling pumps and a varied range of stout and lager fonts. A young, steely-focused barman was seizing the levers, and I admired the way he steered the ship and kept the pub on course.

A 'Wizard' jukebox lit up the wall to my right, and its varying codes of flashing lights and colours, together with its twelve-numbered digit pad, resembled an earth-based Central Control Centre. Turning back to observe the barman, I determined that he was clearly exceptional at his post, but I was only too aware that he would need a more experienced senior officer to direct him through a meteorite shower. Not only this, but would he be up to the task of drinking his own urine when emergency rations became low? Waiting until the patrons had their glasses well topped up, I began waving my goodbyes and blowing kisses before proudly marching around to the back of the bar counter.

Feeling nostalgic as I stood in the midst of the Flight Deck, I motioned my junior pilot over, firmly shaking his hand before briefing him on our mission. The bar patrons who had gathered to watch our departure seemed to lack the keen interest and adrenaline that I housed, and my confused second in command wasn't entirely pleased as he watched me start up the main engines of the ship by flicking all the lager, stout and cider taps to 'On'. His pre-launch nerves were to be expected however, and I instead focused my attention on the voyage ahead; a journey that would soon be underway with a flame-ignited thrusting out of Earth's immediate solar system.

Three rotating pods behind the bar held upended bottles of liquor, and I vigorously twirled and spun these in order to send fuel to the turbine-projected booster rockets. Drops of condensation dripped from the ignition lever taps, and this suggested overheating in the on-board circuitry and a potential hindrance to our textbook lift-off. But there was no time for delays. Violently ringing a conveniently placed small brass bell, I began loudly counting down random numbers in no particular order.

Large clouds of steam were firing out from the dishwasher as I pulled the ale taps firmly back, igniting the jet propulsers, which all going to plan, would later disengage from the craft and land in the sea, somewhere, I forecast, between Brighton and Whitstable. As I waited for the bar area to blast off from the bare wooden floorboards, my eyes were drawn again to the many flyers and leaflets that remained motionless and still on the window-side ledge.

Anticipating engine trouble, I tried to physically lift the bar counter off the ground myself, while anxious members of the public looked on. Squirting whiskey and gin all about my head soon after, I was quickly overpowered by my number two, who, I noticed, had failed to don his regulation white jumpsuit.

Foundry

84-86 Great Eastern Street EC2A 3JL
Nearest tube – Old Street

Unlike most London pubs that pride themselves on traditional charms, the Foundry has taken its leaf from the book of messy bedrooms. Its landmark corner building once housed the more conventional pursuits of banking, but today baby dolls swing from ceiling-suspended wires, a four foot wide chocolate chip biscuit is firmly wedged into an inside wall, and masking tape is stuck all about the place without actually sticking anything. Cables drape over light fittings, microwave ovens are sprayed with graffiti, and the man who served my ale had a head of lime green hair. As I withdrew from the serving area, passing a stuffed human head that was affixed to the woodwork alongside, I resigned myself to the fact that some good old-fashioned darts were not to be forthcoming.

A chunky wooden table is set up like a workbench in the corner of the bar, and after spilling my ale across its rough edged surface area, I began to feel more at one with the chaos strewn around me. After more ales and more spilled drinks, my elbow sleeves were dripping, and I was holding my head like an eggcup when I suddenly became aware of drifting smoke. The man with green hair was lighting fresh candles, and I discovered one protruding from the neck of a wax-covered wine bottle beside me. Attempting to dry my wet sleeves around its flame without success, I decided to head down the steep white block staircase in search of the loos.

The toilet walls in the Gents are covered from floor to ceiling in handwritten, marker pen graffiti, but despite my best efforts I couldn't think of anything clever to add myself because I was stuck with writer's block before the urinals. When I realised I was spending a penny in the basement level of a former bank however, I began imagining lucre that wasn't filthy, but politely stacked in crisp clean bills. Washing my hands with flowing soap from a plastic bottle, I decided to seek out the vaults.

Slightly beyond the toilets in the Foundry's tomb-like depths, I came across a small stark room with modern artworks displayed on its walls. After removing all of these from their hooks in my search for a secret wall safe, I continued empty-handed into a much larger concrete room with a huge circular iron disc in the centre of the floor. Stepping gingerly onto its ribbed surface, I was enthralled to discover that this great old contraption was actually capable of movement. Thrusting it around in a clockwise manner first, I then set it in an opposing direction, attempting all manner of combinations in order to crack the code. No telltale clicks or bleeps were forthcoming however, so I opted for phase two of my plan.

Back upstairs, I stocked up on supplies at the bar before seizing the candle and its wine bottle holder from my dampened workbench table. Descending the staircase again like a glowing nymph, I made my way back to the bowels of the basement. Once seated in a corner of the large concrete room, I carefully removed the flaming candle from the wax-lined neck of the wine bottle, before pouring my freshly acquired vodka into its label-wrapped belly. This done, I then pulled out my creased, ragged old handkerchief and stuffed it deep into the bottle until it was soaked in ridiculously strong alcohol. Lighting the other end of the tatty rag with the still burning candle wick, I waited until the flame had reached well down the neck before I threw it across the room towards the circular iron floor safe.

A large, bright explosion erupted, and I tried to shield my eyes and ears at the same time, like a very fast game of Simon Says. White plaster sprinkled onto my hair and eyebrows, and I walked cautiously towards the pockets of flames, waiting for countless notes of unmarked currency to descend upon my reddened, blackened cheeks.

In retrospect, I probably should have considered the serious nature of the ensuing smoke and fire damage, but fortunately, the local fire station was but a hose-length away on the opposite side of Old Street. Wandering around in a daze with my T-shirt pulled over my face, it wasn't long before I was hauled up as the chief brains and mastermind behind the deed. And when the police started shouting at me soon afterwards, I really wished I still had my ragged old handkerchief to dab at very real tears, but by then it had clearly been reduced to flecks of molten ash.

Golden Heart

110 Commercial Street E1 6LZ
Nearest tube – Liverpool Street

From a distance, the three-storey building which houses the Golden Heart resembles a man's sunburnt head. Its roof is like a clump of hair, the top two storeys are the upper, reddened face, and the ground floor is a five o'clock shadow of stubble.

I entered the Saloon Bar via a set of brown, double-door teeth, finding inside a bustling and convivial crowd. Squeezing amongst the tightly pressed group as if they were invitees to my own party, I nodded to each in acknowledgement, my hearty laughter producing half smiles and blank stares.

The wooden shelving above the bar counter is worth looking out for, as it resembles the small bays on a golf driving range if they were filled with upturned glasses. On the day I happened past, a motorbike helmet sat on top of this shelving, and inside the helmet was a head and it was shouting, but I couldn't hear what exactly because of the loud chatter in the bar. There was a postcard from Pope John Paul II behind the cash register, and to the left, beyond the serving area, I noticed an empty, more secluded bar. Tempted by the thought of a quiet interlude from the party, I vigorously shook the motorbike helmet, motioned a fond farewell to the party guests, and slipped outside in search of the more peaceful spot next door.

The interior of the Golden Heart's Wine Bar was dimly lit, and in comparison to the lively Saloon Bar, it felt more like a room where the guests might leave their coats. The only other person in attendance was a woman with cropped black hair and red-framed glasses who stood in the middle of the room, swivelling a green hula hoop around her hips. A fire crackled at the far end of the room, and I made my way towards the delicatessen style glass bar counter, catching the eye of the bar staff from the busy saloon I'd just left. The lady finished swinging her hoop and proceeded to lift it over her head like a giant pullover before disappearing behind the serving area. Left alone, as if with the coats and umbrellas, I sat silently upon a bench seat, listening to some big-band music from an old-fashioned jukebox at the rear of the small bar room.

Enticed by the sounds of the jukebox and the fire's flickering glow, I decided to move to the back of the Wine Bar and tell myself a ghost story. Feeling like Bruce Wayne in his secret, well-appointed manor house, I held my hands out to the flames and began my tale about a man who dies after seeing his own reflection in a bathroom mirror. I was at the part where the hero character is running his paste-laden toothbrush bristles firmly across his eyes, when I realised I had to visit the toilet.

There were no conveniences on offer in the Wine Bar, so I went back outside to get to the Saloon Bar, finding a door within marked HOMMES. Shortly afterwards, having once again nodded my farewells, I re-entered the Wine Bar, this time noticing that the key to its wooden entrance doors remained in the keyhole, attached to a silver bottle-opener key ring. Without thinking twice, I immediately locked myself inside.

Confident that my secret dual life was now hidden from public view, I approached two plaster busts that illuminated a brown piano near the entrance door and turned the right hand bust 360 degrees. As if on cue, the piano beneath suddenly transformed into a jet-propelled rocket car, and removing the lid I climbed inside with my drink.

It's hard to adequately describe my journey around the East End of London inside the Piano Car because I was travelling so fast and my eyes were closed. My trip was interrupted sooner than I'd hoped however, by the sound of rattling doors. Footsteps entered the bar room from behind the serving area, along with voices of confusion and words describing my sex, age and height in raised tones. Thinking that my butler was trying to reach me in order to relay an important message, I loudly wallowed around on the wooden piano keys, shouting: "I'M INSIDE THE PIANO CAR, BUT I'M NOT WEARING MY MASK."

When the car roof was lifted up by the barwoman and my true identity was exposed, I tried to make a quick getaway, but my mistake was attempting to start up the Piano Car with the key to the Golden Heart's Wine Bar door.

Ye Old Mitre

1 Ely Court, Ely Place EC1N 6SJ
Nearest tube – Chancery Lane / Farringdon

Ye Old Mitre is one of London's finest historic pubs, and if you put the time in to find it, the rewards reaped will be great. Prior to my expedition, very wise people had cautioned me in regards to its elusive nature, and this knowledge proved to be well founded when, at one point, my forehead veins were bulging like fingers wriggling around inside a thin nylon sock.

I began my search in Ely Place, a strange private street with a sentry post manned by a uniformed guard. Tank turrets may have been trained on me as I looked in vain for a swinging pub sign or a quick glimpse of Tony Blair or Winston Churchill. But seeing neither, I strayed instead to Hatton Garden where, after a further fruitless search, I was lured by the bright yellow colours of a photo-processing shop. Inside, happily pointing at the name badges on each staff members' respective chest and reciting them aloud, I explained that I was an amateur photographer myself, with a special interest in litter and Christmas themes. After using up 23 disposable cameras, taking photos of my ears for trial purposes, one of the very pleasant staff members stormed off to hunt down the whereabouts of the Ye Old Mitre for me, causing the shop's hanging mobiles to swing wildly in the gust from the slamming door.

A short time later I was shaking the white-gloved hands of my photographic laboratory friends, thanking them for their hospitality and guidance, before departing with a partially used disposable camera that they insisted I should keep.

A sturdy sign mounted on a short, old-fashioned lamppost provided the telltale steer to Ye Old Mitre pub, pointing down an alleyway that linked Hatton Garden with Ely Place. A sign above the narrow brick passage denoted that Ye Old Mitre was EST in 1546, and entering the dark enclave I observed an impressively heaped mound of pigeon droppings, the foundations of which had probably first been laid a day or so before. When I finally laid eyes on Ye Old Mitre, it appeared like a hidden cottage made of candy within a deep, mysterious wood. Pretty plants provided decorative forest cover for the windows outside, and I made my way towards an old wooden door marked LOUNGE BAR, its 20 small square windows covered in a variety of flyers and stickers.

Inside, a warm and welcoming atmosphere predominated, and my eyes soaked in the dark wood-panelled interior like little soggy clumps of yellow-white bread bait. A cosy fireplace burnt away quietly as I suggested an ale from the young, smartly attired barman, and with this in hand, I walked across traditional pub carpet before seating myself upon a lovely old chair with a carved back that resembled an onion. Looking about me, I noticed that most of the furniture appeared to have been pulled, as if magnetically, towards the perimeter walls. This observation was confirmed by a sign near the servery that read: WOULD CUSTOMERS KINDLY REFRAIN FROM MOVING FURNITURE AWAY FROM THE WALLS, and I imagined the solid thwack of wood as each taken piece was sucked back at pace to its wall position.

Drinking quickly to make up for lost time, I made my way back towards the bar, imagining a bungee cord was strapped securely around my waist. I slowly struggled over with giant-like heavy strides, as if walking through a pool of chunky fish chowder. Other patrons broke their conversations to watch me, no doubt impressed by the example I was setting by returning my empty glass to the servery, saving the bar staff the unneeded chore involved with its collection.

Finally reaching the small, cake-bake-stall-like serving area, I again placed my order, making quite a show of returning my glass with its faint smear of my lips and saliva. A second sign caught my eye, which read: IF YOU THINK THE HEAD ON YOUR BEER IS TOO LARGE TELL US. WE WILL GLADLY TOP UP YOUR GLASS. I judged my new pint to be poured to perfection, but as I released my white-knuckled gripping hand from its clutch on the bar top, I was suddenly flung back in the direction of my onion chair at a velocity that made my cheeks flap like wind-swept pudding. My drink waved around my head like a spinning lasso rope, and as I slammed against the wall near my seat, the remaining contents of my pint splattered around my head as if I'd just placed a rifle in my mouth and blown out a bloodstream comprised of ale.

I returned my second empty glass to the bar counter with the same effort-filled stride, this time escorted by the smartly dressed man whose task I'd saved, and I managed to take a quick photo of his angry face because he wasn't wearing a name badge.

Ye Olde Cheshire Cheese

145 Fleet Street EC4A 2BU
Nearest tube – Blackfriars tube/rail

Ye Olde Cheshire Cheese is one of London's most famous pubs, and also one of its oldest. A pub has stood on its site since the 16th century at least, and the current premises were rebuilt in 1667 after the Great Fire of the previous year. While many historic inns and taverns have chosen to 'move with the times', remodelling themselves on the stage sets from children's television programmes, Ye Olde Cheshire Cheese has thankfully retained its features, its character and its good old-fashioned sense.

The dark wooden interior features an enchanting warren of narrow corridors and staircases, and I hoped I wouldn't run into my high school history teacher because he might have sent me outside again, and it was raining. My wet shoes collected sawdust that had been sprinkled about the floor, and after securing a pint of ale, I settled within a small dark room known as the Gentleman's Bar, finding a seat to the right of the fireplace.

With shoes resembling Worzel Gummidge's feet, thanks to the accumulated sawdust, I stretched my legs like a pub gymnast and began to wonder about the other shoes that had clomped around these same slated floors as I. Charles Dickens was a regular in his time, and his well-polished buckle-strap cobblers, tainted as they no doubt were with the putrid stench of Victorian London, had surely preceded my very steps. Other famous patrons, such as Boswell, Johnson, Thackeray, Chesterton and Doyle must have graced the very slabs also, noisily stomping as if to say, 'LOOK AT ME, I'M A CELEBRITY. I'M IN THE PAPERS.'

My Dad has some old brown shoes that he uses in the garden, and I was sure that at some point in history, a man who owned the exact same style and fit came into this very pub and walked around. Recent tourists would surely have pressed substantial weight upon white-patterned soles that have first touched spilled soda on plastic floors in chain restaurants. Fluffy slippers with animal heads on the front. It seemed more than plausible to me that at least one person had strode within this distinguished establishment over the many centuries past with large fluffy giraffe heads for shoes.

I compiled a personal list comprising over 1400 possible footwear combinations that had strode around this great London tavern, and as I yabbered aloud, smelling the insides of my own trainers, I began working out where all these footsteps had actually been placed within the bar area. Passageways seemed obvious, stairs, spaces immediately beneath chairs and stools, and of course the waiting areas in front of the bar counters. At the same time however, this also meant that there was likely to be a lot of floor area that very few people had actually stepped upon, if in fact, anyone at all.

After proceeding around to the rear Cheshire Bar, I began thrusting my shoe-enshrouded feet onto every possible space beneath the radiators. Moving the lathed wooden bar tables into the centre of the bar area, I then stood plonk, plonk on all the previously covered floor space here as well. Next, I removed my shoes and placed my bare hands inside them instead. Crouching down on all fours, I proceeded to crawl beneath the old wooden bench pews, stamping my footwear-gloved hands on the infrequently shoe-touched floor. Big-grinned and clapping my shoe hands, I wandered around to the Chop Room dining area out front. The diners were seated at large wooden tables enjoying tasty lamb shanks and other fine cuisine as I stomped my shoe-covered hands beneath their comfortably seated rumps.

Small sawdust flakes continued to cling to my footwear, until I suddenly exclaimed: "NO YOU BIG LUMP! THAT'S NOT SAWDUST! THAT'S GRATED CHEESE!" Of course! Visitors were encouraged to scurry around and eat all the cheese off the floor like starving orphan children! I slapped my forehead hard and laughed. And then off I went, scurry, scurry, scurry, chomp, chomp, chomp on Ye Olde Cheshire Cheese's floor-scattered grated cheese.

The taste was a little peculiar, but I took into account that it was probably olde and past its expiry date by about two hundred years. It sure filled me up, that floor-scattered cheese, and I was feeling a little under the weather when I was suddenly hoisted up off the ground and flung out into the narrow alleyway beside the entrance door. One of my red and white canvas shoes bounced off my head, and I swear it was my history teacher's voice that loudly resounded: "AND DON'T COME BACK, YOU LITTLE FREAK!"

Three Kings of Clerkenwell

7 Clerkenwell Close EC1R ODY
Nearest tube – Farringdon

The Three Kings is situated directly opposite St. James, a church with stained glass window designs clearly borrowed from that of the traditional English pub. I only witnessed two people come and go through its large and imposing doors all afternoon, while the Three Kings was, in comparison, doing a brisk and steady trade.

A fine selection of ales, together with many other varieties of alcohol and a rhinoceros head are, one must say, formidable challenges to the church in the early years of the 21st century, although there is obviously much to say for rich purple tapestries and dried rotting bones that are buried on your surrounding grounds. My pew in the Three Kings was at a table which ran directly alongside the open footpath, the red doors to the street having being pulled back, as if to tempt those straying from the righteous path. From here I could keep an all-seeing eye on St. James' church, while still inspecting the many fine details of the pub I was within.

Although prosperous in good old-fashioned pub atmosphere, the Three Kings also gives a subtle nod to modern decor with earthy paint tones in shades of mustard and beetroot, and lighting that is projected through an eclectic range of lampshades, tubes, Christmas lights and art boxes. A TV mounted high on the wall is fairly contemporary also, and it was tuned into a bicycle race when I glanced up, but fortunately the sound was turned down because no one likes the sound of rubber tread on road. To the right of this, mounted above a fireplace, is a rhino head, and I assumed the rest of its body was facing the other side of this wall, in some side room.

A small clear glass ashtray on my table resembled a scale prototype for a futuristic botanical glasshouse that would host ferns and multi-coloured butterflies when inverted, and this was on my mind when a passing car disturbed my pleasant outing in the Three Kings. It was driving fairly slowly, and it was not particularly erratic or noisy, but it left behind an arid pong of smoky exhaust fumes. Waiting until it had driven around the corner, I raised my fist and shook it, and when the noise of the engine failed to reach me, I shouted: "YOU FILTHY MURDERING BASTARD!" Soon after another vehicle passed by and the sensitive olfactory hairs within my nose were once again defiled. Downing my pint of ale, I decided to shift my table and chair out into the middle of the road.

My wooden chair was lightly varnished, resembling a chair that has been briefly dipped in boiling fat, and I carried it across the concrete paving-blocked pavement and out onto the narrow, tarmacked roadway, before returning for my table. Nine pints of ale soon stretched across the road like spikes, and I sat on my bar chair wearing my handkerchief across my nose and mouth like Dick Turpin.

The first car that approached was a silver SUV vehicle, and the red-faced driver was forced to break suddenly when he encountered the table and the pint glasses and my cold, accusatory eyes. Raising his own Sellotape-yellow eyes in exasperation, he pressed his hands firmly down, as if to detonate tightly packed explosives, causing instead a loud parp noise.

The engine revved furiously, and putrid, deathly fumes began to squirm like tadpoles beneath my handkerchief in a frantic rush for my nostrils. Already driven to an agitated state by the piercing sound of the horn, I now detected clearly hostile signals from an encroaching aggressor, and snorting, I prepared to charge. Stepping carefully over the pints of ale, I stomped my foot awkwardly in a knee-raising way before running at a tremendous pace towards the vehicle with my head lowered.

When I came round, a barman from the Three Kings was dabbing my face and forehead with an ice-cold cloth, and I'd like to present this cloth to St. James' church as a shroud of sorts, but I'll need to give it a good wash first because it's still covered in dried blood and bits of scabby skin.

East

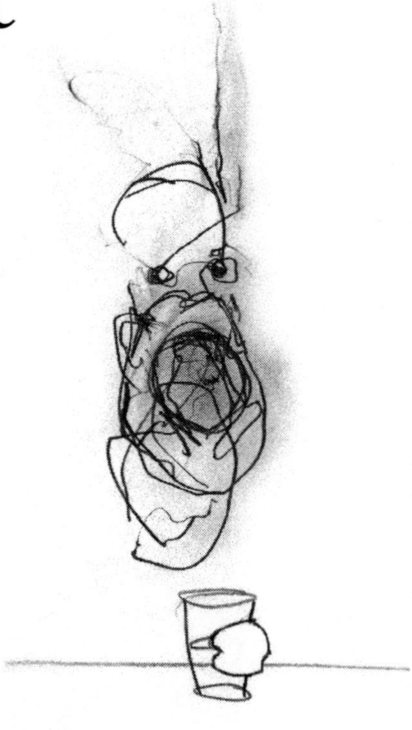

Blind Beggar

337 Whitechapel Road E1 1BU
Nearest tube – Whitechapel

If you walk to the Blind Beggar during market hours, your senses will be assaulted by a vast array of wondrous colours and smells. Purple sari fabric and cyan peppers transform Whitechapel into a visual and olfactory feast, and fresh produce tempts the taste buds from beneath blue and white stripy tarpaulins.

It was a particularly hot London day as I navigated my way through the crowds of shoppers and browsers, and the beads on my forehead were wet and dribbly when compared with the small exotic decorative pieces that were attached to thin lengths of knotted string. As I slowly made my passage, a brightly coloured floor rug happened to catch my eye, and I haggled briefly with the moustachioed vendor before settling upon a reasonable fee for a roll of his trestle-tabled wares.

Arriving outside the Blind Beggar a short time later, I found myself baring witness to a most deplorable scene. A perfectly innocent gentleman was departing through the doors of the pub, and I watched aghast as he was suddenly struck in the face, his glasses shattered, and his forehead lashed with tightly weaved fibres. It was a pointless act of random violence, and I apologised profusely before slinking quickly inside.

The drooping tulip light shades in the Blind Beggar create an atmosphere best described as ominous. It was through this gloom that I observed two large black and white portrait photos of Ronnie and Reggie Kray, the former having gained much notoriety after gunning a man down in this very pub back in 1966. After returning from the bar, I sat uneasily beneath each photograph on a battered and torn leather couch seat, watching helplessly as a tiny bar fly struggled about on the surface of my recently acquired ale.

A large brick fireplace presided to my right, clearly dormant due to the unusually hot weather that permeated the surroundings. But realising I'd need a fair old blaze to get my cigar going, I produced a box of matches and set the tidy assortment of logs and kindling alight until the flames were leaping. A man on his way to the Gents eyed me with suspicion, pausing to watch as I inserted my cylindrical tapestry into the flames and began sucking furiously on its opposing end. The unfiltered tip was the same circumference as my entire face, and despite inhaling absolutely nothing, the tightly packed head was at least well ablaze as I made my way back to my armchair with pungent clouds of black smoke billowing everywhere.

I was using two hands to hold my cigar in front of my head, like a packed blowpipe capable of firing small dogs, when I became aware of a damp stain soaking my left breast. A darkened patch on my light cottoned shirt was congealing quickly in the balmy heat of the day, and as my breath quickened into a raspy gasping, my vision blurred into a series of kaleidoscopic waves that resembled cross-knit jumper patterns. Barely able to stand, I staggered around, drowning in sweat, swinging my flaming cigar wildly and displacing a framed oil painting of sailing ships that had previously hung with distinction above the fireplace.

"YOU DIRTY RAT BASTARD!" I screamed with tightly closed eyes, and mystified staff and patrons rushed through the dense dark clouds of smoke in order to try and stem the flow from my heart. They were clearly outraged by modern gangster activity in the very clean and well maintained bar area, and I continued to shout loudly, gritting and gnashing my teeth, as a particularly brave individual hero carefully removed a slick blue stationary shop biro from my chest pocket, dangling it about, confused.

The modest everyday heroes of the Blind Beggar pub began dragging me outside towards some clear breathing air, and on the way I caught a glimpse of the bar fly whose life had now ended in my pint. Smiling weakly, I ventured with firm resolve that if I pulled through I would one day return to the Blind Beggar to view their life-sized bronze sculpture of me.

Nag's Head

9 Orford Road E17 9LP
Nearest tube – Walthamstow Central

Many Londoners head to Spain or Greece in summer, but the smart ones stay in town and sit outside in garden bars like the Nag's Head. I did, and I sat by myself at a round table with a silver fish-scale top. I had been allocated three alloy chairs with flax-style seating and backing, and if other sun-worshippers had wished to join me for a glass of guest ale, they would, of course, have been welcomed with nervous, spluttering laughter. As it happened, my only visitors were leaves falling from the over-hanging tree above, and I only pressed these between the rear pages of my diary book when I was quite certain I wasn't being watched.

My visit had begun inside at the bar where small signs above the counter read: PLEASE MIND YOUR HEAD. As a rule of thumb, you should also mind your bags and jackets, because I've found that thieves operate even in nice pubs. The garden bar is behind the serving area to the right, and I walked through a rear door into a white canvas tent with walls made of clear, wrinkled plastic. A further opening led outside where I encountered tall silver heaters resembling long-necked robots wearing safari hats. Christmas-style lights wrapped around trees and hung across their branches, and a sign on the rear brick wall read: PLEASE RESPECT OUR NEIGHBOURS. PLEASE KEEP NOISE TO A MINIMUM AFTER

11:00PM. THANKYOU. This impressed me a lot because I know us bar patrons can be a rowdy bunch, and I remember once I overheard this old guy tell a particularly funny joke in a quiet residential pub, and I laughed and laughed really loudly like a horse and the old man and a few of his friends and the bar staff looked across to me and said: "HEY, WHY DON'T YOU SHUT YOUR CAKE HOLE?"

It got me thinking that maybe I should pop next door to one of the neighbour's houses and speak to them about the Nag's Head in order to get their spin on the place. This would clearly break new ground in pub reviewing, and so I decided to clamber up onto the wooden decking structure in the right hand corner of the garden bar area and use it to prop myself over the white brick wall into the neighbour's back yard.

To do this, I first had to navigate a thin wooden bench, which was already occupied by a small group of pub patrons. Nodding good-naturedly, I peeled between them, as if they were dense undergrowth, and made my ascent. Regrettably, my foot struck one gentleman about the head, and there was a lot of indignation voiced as I scrambled out of reach of his grasping hands and hoisted myself over the wall. Brushing myself off, I strode across to the back door of the neighbour's house and rapped my knuckles on it confidently, fishing my pen and notebook out of my bag in preparation for some speedy note taking.

There was no reply, but the kitchen window was slightly ajar, so I decided I would climb through it and leave a questionnaire for the occupants behind one of the fridge magnets. I must have put my clumsy shoes on that day because I accidentally put one of them right through the windowpane and also splintered the varnished wooden frame. Rather than risk cutting myself, I kicked out the remaining glass shards and clambered through.

As I wandered throughout the house, I paused in each room to check on the level of noise wafting over from the Nag's Head garden bar. In order to be very thorough, I also made my tests with the shower running, with the TV and stereo volumes turned up, and from beneath the pulled up sheets and duvets of all the beds.

I had a pillowcase over my head and was loudly gargling wine, when suddenly there was a noisy commotion near the back door. I ran blindly with my arms outstretched, before being pinned to the lino floor by a large weight. Attempting to lighten the situation, I recited the joke I'd once heard that old man tell, repeating the punch line with extra emphasis and laughter as an unfaltering voice continued to read me my rights.

Prince George

40 Parkholme Road E8 3AG
Nearest tube – Hackney Downs rail/Dalston Kingsland rail

I was seated at the far end of a long wooden pew the day I visited the Prince George pub, and noticing two other wooden pews facing me from the opposite wall, I rather imagined I was sitting in a psychiatrist's waiting room. Most of the varnish had been scraped off the small table surface before me, and this, I deciphered, was undoubtedly the work of mad people.

My bench and table were situated in a rear section of the bar, and on the wall to my left was a large movie poster depicting a scene from the film La Dolce Vita. The poster featured an image of a woman holding up a cat, and on the wall beside it was a framed black and white photograph of another woman who was also holding up a cat. You have to have a cat to get on the wall of the Prince George I concluded, and ever hopeful, I walked with the air of Dick Whittington on my way back to the bar.

After ordering a pint of ale from the psychiatrist, I told her about a dream I'd had where I was being chased by giant hair-curlers through an abandoned fairground. I couldn't escape from the hair-curlers, I told her, because my legs were made from spicy sausage meat. She nodded sympathetically before turning to another customer with raised eyebrows, and I gave them both my funny cross-eyed expression before making my way back across the wooden floorboards, as if wearing large clown shoes.

To the immediate left of my table was a small black cupboard that was no higher than three feet tall and equally limited in width. I couldn't open it at first because my wooden pew was hard up against the door, so I began shunting the long bench seat along in order to create some space outside it. I was the only one sitting in this rear bar area at the time, and no one noticed as I squatted down, pried the little door ajar and climbed inside, pulling it shut behind me.

I sat hunched in the dark with my pint of ale waiting for people to sit at the table outside. It was very cramped, but there was a lovely musty smell from the encroaching walls, and it felt like night time even though it was the middle of the afternoon. I started making loud sucking noises to entertain myself, some of which were really, really funny, and at one point I laughed so much I coughed up some ale through my nose. Eventually, after a couple of hours or so, I heard some footsteps and voices right outside the cupboard door announcing the arrival of some patrons at my table. They were talking about some interesting topic of the moment and as they weren't scraping the varnish off the table surface or sounding particularly mad, I knew I was pretty safe hiding inside a tiny cupboard right next to them.

Wetting my lips, I began to play a few quiet chords from the harmonica I had managed to retrieve from my rear trouser pocket. I've never pretended to be a particularly accomplished harmonica player, and in fact all I really do is run my lips back and forth really fast and blow. A noisy, shrill frenzy of harmonics soon reverberated inside my tiny wooden den, and I'd like to think I pulled off a fairly convincing interpretation of 'Rhythm is a Dancer.' A subsequent hush emerged from the people immediately outside, and when the little door was suddenly whisked back, I was temporarily blinded by the bright daylight that flooded the interior of the Prince George pub.

I thought about arranging another appointment with my psychiatrist as I was escorted, meowing, towards the doors, but she asked me not to return, YOU LITTLE HAIR-CURLER, SAUSAGE-MEAT FREAK!

North

Dublin Castle

94 Parkway NW1 7AN
Nearest tube – Camden Town

Many live bands of repute have cut their teeth within the walls of the Dublin Castle pub, and I managed to leave with all my teeth polished and intact, despite some minor bruising to my face and ears.

It was a bright, sunny afternoon when I made my way into the dimly lit surroundings, and walking with the sophisticated vision of a short-tailed fruit bat, I sought out an ale from the bar. The overall ambience actually reminded me of the alien bar in Star Wars, and this observation seemed verified by the pierced faces, weird clothes and outrageous hairstyles of the Camden locals. They all appeared to be smoking like the smashed windows of a high school struck by arson, but they paid me no mind as I drunk my ale through my mouth, rather than sucking it out of my glass by way of an index finger. Happy to play the part of the outcast Luke Skywalker character who just wants to fit in with the freaks, I patted my trouser pocket, finding not the cylindrical bulge of a trusty lightsaber, but the pressed square mound of a folded linen handkerchief.

The stage and performance area, where many a musical legend has been forged, is situated in a separate back area, past two glass-panelled wooden doors, but feeling I had little to prove, I opted for the front of the bar and a faded blue upholstered bench that curved around a small table. Leaning back on my sofa seat, thinking that an edgy name for a hot new band could be 'Urine Joss Stick', I noticed a crumpled up tissue on one of the wooden floorboards. It didn't make a huge impression on me at first, and I looked away instead towards the more interesting flyers and posters that were stuck to the wall of mirrors behind me. But when I looked back across the bar again, I was surprised to notice that the tissue had now moved significantly across the floor towards my table. Strangely, the area it had covered on its journey now appeared dry and free of the drips that plagued other parts of the floor.

Putting two and two together, I realised that the tissue was scooting around mopping up all the random drops of spilt beer. It was clearly embedded with some sort of electronic sensor and had been programmed to detect drips and splashes caused by well-topped up glasses. Connected to a tiny battery pack, this electronic sensor was no doubt wired up to a complex hydraulics system, which in turn powered a small motor that fed the sophisticated navigational equipment.

I couldn't hear a whirr sound emanating from the tissue (due perhaps to the bustling chatter that resonated within the bar), and I stared at it for ages and it didn't move an inch. "WHAT A BRILLIANT INVENTION!" I voiced aloud, attempting to register my appreciation with the staff. It was about this time that I noticed the barstools, which were positioned alongside the serving counter. Some of these were of a modern style with black seats and metal stands, and their circular footrests reminded me of the round door handles on submarines. The electronic sensor tissue would have a real test of its ability if it had to soak up the entire ocean, I thought, and so I walked across the gleaming floorboards with my pint of ale and placed it on the ground beside one of the barstools.

Upon this particular stool sat an older, solidly built man; his vast array of tattoos featuring snakes and women with bare and brazen breasts. I squatted on the floor beside his generous hips, squeezing his large lad's knee in a quietly confiding manner. He responded with an outburst of some kind, but I couldn't quite catch what he said due to a brief, deafening blare of very innovative live music that erupted through the opened rear bar doors. Grasping the circular, watertight hatch on his stool, I began turning it furiously in an anti-clockwise motion, causing him to rotate around and face the opposite direction from his adjacent friend. It was a fair old heave-ho trying to release an ocean of salt water into the smoke-filled surroundings of the Dublin Castle, and somewhat out of breath, I attempted to fend off a large hairy hand that was grasping the neckline of my T-shirt. The whale of a man remained firmly seated on the door hatch, and I was forced to defend myself as he begun lashing out with his large, blubbery arms and hands.

I was attempting to explain to him about the genius behind the electronic sensor tissue when, a short time later, we were being driven to the police station, not in an X-34 Landspeeder hovering aloft on a cushion of antigravity, but in a plain white Rover automobile with ordinary tyres.

Flask

77 Highgate West Hill N6 6BU
Nearest tube – Highgate

The Flask is a vast, early eighteenth century pub, nestled on the edge of Highgate Hill, and a hearty welcome is extended to both young and old within.

Many low-ceilinged rooms and compartments fill the large and sprawling bar area, and one is offered a multitude of choices for sofas, seats and stools. My ridiculously bad posture was supported upon the ornate wooden base of a luxurious red leather couch, while opposite, a young tortoiseshell cat lay upon a wooden bench pew casually cleaning its forearms. A distinct lack of piped music or television commentary made for a peaceful afternoon setting, until this tranquil scene was suddenly shredded by a piercing sound that reverberated loudly off the wood-panelled walls.

The hollers and screams of a small baby are never a pleasant soundtrack to the savouring of a tasty real ale, and as the noise increased within the mild-mannered Flask, the young cat sat up on its haunches, worried by the rowdy element that now threatened the pub calm and serenity. Deciding more booze was needed to combat this onslaught to the ears, I made a run to the bar, returning soon afterwards with another pint of ale and a fresh saucer of creamy milk. The cry-baby noise continued unabated, and as the cat licked its small, puckered bottom, I decided a plan was needed to restore peace to the Flask of Highgate pub. Clapping my hands to catch the cat's eye of the cat, I grinned and winked knowingly. Then, wiping the dribbles of milk from my unshaven chin, I raised the saucer above my head and smashed it down upon the wooden fireside table.

'I'M IN TROUBLE NOW!' I thought, as I raced off like a maniac in the direction of the baby's noisy wail. Its parents were noticeably surprised as I came sliding across the dry wooden floorboards, and when I attempted to slither up the gentleman's trouser leg he caught me sharply across the nose with the back of his hand. My pupils began rolling around my eye sockets like marbles in a pint glass, and my tongue curled out of the side of my mouth in a limp and dopey fashion. Shaking my head like a dusty sock, my darting eyes began searching for my furry pursuer, fearing he was ready to pounce.

There was no sign of him at all actually, and so I ran like the clappers through the bar, looking for a hole in the skirting board or a bendy knife that I could catapult salt and pepper shakers with. I'm quite sure the baby had stopped crying when I sent an orange string lampshade crashing to the floor, and startled patrons in the rear rooms looked on aghast as I clambered across their wooden chest tables, upsetting drinks and intimate words. Ashtrays were thrown randomly over my shoulder, causing paint chips to displace from the curved, bunker-like ceiling, but the cat wasn't in hot pursuit, or even a pleasant mild variant.

I was still racing about with my large ears pinned back as I reached the raised bar serving area at the top of a small flight of stairs. Snatching a host of condiments from a wooden bench, I squeezed their respective sauces all about me before feeling the urge to roll about in flour.

"I WANT TO ROLL ABOUT IN CLOUDS OF FLOUR!" I called excitedly to the barmaid, but she immediately turned her back on me and continued with her important phone call.

"THE QUIET AND FRIENDLY TORTOISESHELL CAT IS TO BLAME," I told the two policemen, and one of them shook his head sadly as he wrote into a small lined notebook. My well-groomed friend had disappeared completely at this point however, and I felt a twang of guilt, suspecting he was out in the kitchen being whacked with a large old-fashioned broom.

Harringay Arms

153 Crouch Hill N8 9QH
Nearest tube – Crouch Hill rail

The Harringay Arms is a small and cosy Crouch End pub, modestly placed near the base of Crouch Hill, and on the overcast Saturday I happened by, it was filled with silence, occasional rustles and placid old gents. Some of the patrons were seated quietly in twos at the bar, others watched the televised horse racing out back, but for the most part they were reading the weekend papers, surrounded by snugs of newsprint.

At the rear of the bar, a well-used coat rack is mounted for your convenience on the wall below the television, and to the right of this is a framed illustration of the bar interior. An older man was watching the horses with a green pen lodged firmly behind his ear, and when the racing coverage was rudely disrupted by advertising material, he produced a remote control to mute the sound and reinstall some common sense.

It was during one such quiet spell that a low, deep rumble was heard to emerge from the basement water pipes of my stomach. The other bar patrons heard it also, and somewhat embarrassed, I pretended that a wide-load truck had just passed outside on Crouch Hill, my hands making a show of gripping a large steering wheel before adjusting an imaginary rear view mirror. As the raised straggly eyebrows turned slowly back to the day's headlines, I accepted the harsh fact that I hadn't actually eaten anything since the previous day. I was feeling fairly ravenous and so I began to rub my belly, scanning the tables around me for pork scratching leftovers, or crumbs of bacon bits. And then I noticed the man with a head like a fish.

His body was perched on light crimson barstool cushioning, and his head was slightly hidden behind the walls of large newspaper pages. I watched as he turned the pages with a sound that resembled a shaken box of matches, and it was then he revealed his bulging eyes, each covered in a watery film that threatened to splish and slosh. I stared at his gills and his fat, slimy lips, and I felt like an urchin of the street who has his hands and greedy face pressed up to the window of a seafood takeaway. He was sitting just a few feet away, and carefully studying his face, I concluded that it most certainly resembled the succulent face of a fish. A fresh, delicious cod in fact. Good pub food, cod. I was salivating like a bathroom mirror after a particularly hot shower, and setting my pint glass down with a clonk noise, I moved towards Mr. Fish Head, licking and smacking my chops.

His earlobes seemed particularly out of place for a fish, and I was looking for vinegar and other condiments as I attempted to wrap him up inside his newspaper. It was important that I wrapped him tightly, I thought, in order to seal in the heat and freshness. Then, once comfortably back behind my small round table, I could rip a small hole in the paper and dip my hand in for a...chip. WHERE WERE THE CHIPS?

My nose began sniffing about for chips, while my hands struggled desperately to rein in the old gent's torso and legs, which were leaping about within the Jobs & Money pages. As his barstool was sent crashing to the floor, an eruption of crinkled newspaper resounded throughout the pub, followed by a thundering stampede of old dependable shoes. I was wrestled to the floor by strong, white-haired, age-spotted arms, and the first carpet burns were applied to my nose just as the horses burst through the gate in the eighth at Sandown Park.

Holly Bush

22 Holly Mount NW3 6SG
Nearest tube – Hampstead

Liam Gallagher from Oasis turned up at the Holly Bush the day I visited. I was attempting to choose from the selection of ales at the bar when he walked in with a mate, requesting alcoholic beverages in a decisive manner. His friend looked as though he'd won a breakfast cereal competition to have a drink with Liam Gallagher in Hampstead, so blanking him, I stared instead at Liam while loudly jangling the coins and keys inside my pockets. His famous leather cap formed a brim across his forehead, and his sunglasses reflected my own teeth and head, and my limp shoulders that resembled the broken wings of a small bird.

I don't write music reviews, but I have written about pubs that have music playing in them, and although I prefer pubs that are quiet and music-free, I was quite sure the ones I visited that played Oasis songs were very good indeed. I decided I'd mention this to Liam immediately, and I also wanted to ask him how you get to be one of those people who carry the different guitars onto the stage at the really big concerts. But his lagers arrived before I'd made my choice of ale, and as the two of them walked off towards the rear of the bar, I walked quickly on the spot, filling my mouth with my knuckles.

Oak flooring and extensive wood panelling play a dominant role in the layout of the pub interior, which was originally a stable block built in the mid 17th century. It was converted into a tavern in the early 1800's, and the original gas lamps.......Just then the barmaid presented me with my well-poured pint, and waving off my change, I half-ran out back, eager to explore the many intricate passageways and rooms of the Holly Bush.

Liam and company were sitting in the first side room I came across and I decided to park there awhile and check it out. I didn't purposefully sit at the same table as them, but it was a very long bench, and I was inspecting it for character, cleanliness and height. When I started laughing out loud to myself, the other two suddenly stopped talking. I can't quite remember why I started laughing, but I think it had something to do with a very funny whorl in the wood. I was still laughing, really laughing, as my foot began tapping loudly on the floorboards, like a robotic dancing foot. Shuddering vibrations ran up my leg as I banged out my tune, and the metal clip on my pen began its accompaniment by forcefully striking the tabletop to form a vague Da da da da, da da da da tune of sorts. Still laughing, I began loudly humming along, and it was about then that Liam introduced himself.

He didn't say, "HELLO, I'M LIAM GALLAGHER, WHAT'S YOUR NAME?" Nothing formal like that. In fact, his keenness for conversation impressed me, because usually when I sit in pubs by myself, nervously staring at everyone with wide, frightened eyes, no one even looks my way. But Liam wasn't like that. Instead, he was very open and forthcoming in his constructive criticism towards my amateur composition.

I was silent for a while after that.

On the wall behind me was a picture of the artist George Romney who bought the stables (and adjoining house) that were later to become the Holly Bush, way back in 1796. His pose was most dignified, and he seemed to nod approvingly as I climbed up onto the wooden table.

"I'M ON STAGE, I'M ON STAGE, I'M ON STAGE NOW!!"

My head was contorted as I shouted and danced around in a frenetic, awkward way, causing drinks to overturn, glasses to smash, and voices to be raised like triangular-shaped guitars.

As I was escorted out by a member of staff, I caught a whiff of roast chicken with barley-mustard stuffing, sautéed potatoes and minted courgette, and I decided I'd get room service to bring some of this up to my suite, and also loads of chocolate and fifty pints of lager.

Island Queen

87 Noel Road N1 8HD
Nearest tube – Angel

Islington has a fairly generous sprinkling of well-preserved boozers, and you'll be desperate to reach them after travelling on the longest escalator system in the entire London Underground network.

The Island Queen isn't the closest pub to Angel tube station, nestled as it is along the quiet residential back street of Noel Road, and I was staggering and sweaty as I approached it, causing the local inhabitants to look up from their outdoor tables as if I'd just emerged dripping from the ocean waves. After pausing to admire the magnificent etched glass Victorian exterior, I shuffled my way inside, finding fans circling overhead and palm decorations that appeared to melt like green cheese onto large impressive mirrors.

Collecting a pint of refreshing ale from the island bar, I made my way towards a small, partially enclosed room at the rear, seating myself upon a long wooden bench seat with ornately carved ski-jump armrests. Framed prints of colonial ships suggested a nautical theme, a point heightened by an original, full-size figurehead that had been taken from its post on a bow of a ship and placed alongside the door to the Ladies' toilet. Although beautifully crafted, time had unfortunately rendered the piece somewhat worse for wear. Her nose and forearms were missing, determined knees appeared to be gnawing through her flowing gown, and her square slab base was badly chipped like a mouse-nibbled slab of wax. Candles flickered throughout the bar, and I imagined this figurehead as a giant candle herself, warning lighthouses about her approach via a glowing chin or a flaming set of illuminated ears.

As she cast her eyes across this charming neighbourhood bar, rather than the salt-lipped waves and exotic shores she'd once navigated, it did enter my mind that perhaps the smell of toilet freshener simply couldn't replace the wafts of salt, seaweed and sailors that had permeated her past, and now the great dame of the oceans was longing for some small temporary reminder of her daring ocean life. Finishing my ale, I walked back to the bar and ordered eleven more.

Lining the pints up along a table beside the wondrous edifice to the shifting seas, I began heaving them one by one into her face, slamming each drained glass back down like some rowdy old buccaneer.

"SQUARK, SQUARK!"

Squatting down, I flapped my arms around like a seagull's wings and waddled through the bar as if I were dipping and weaving through a strong coastal breeze.

SPLISH, SPLASH!

I doused the old figurine with yet another pint before physically grabbing her heavy wooden frame, rocking it back and forth in an attempt to recreate the swirling motions of the mighty ocean swell.

The chime-like light fittings began to rattle, as if to signal the first signs of an approaching storm, and I watched helplessly as the vast weight of the old figurehead tipped forward and crashed down on top of me, pinning my small delicate body to the ground and crushing the wind right out of my sails.

A bewildered and mystified crowd stood around us, their hands on their hips as they muttered strictly land-based comments about my thoughtful deeds. When the police arrived soon after, everyone helped wrench the great weight from my wreck of a body and blue face. And as the paramedics stretchered me out of the Island Queen, I couldn't help but think that the old dame, despite her lack of forearms, had somehow been trying to embrace me for my caring and insightful gesture.

O'Reilly's

289-291 Kentish Town Road NW5 2JS
Nearest tube – Kentish Town

Although Irish pubs play a major role in London's drinking landscape, many of the recent offerings resemble hastily erected movie sets and one-dimensional facades. Exceptions to this rule include some very fine boozers indeed however, and for a slice of the genuine crac, try O'Reilly's in Kentish Town.

On the day I happened by, living breathing Irish folk were enjoying conversation, laughter and drinks, and I took this as a healthy sign of the pub's authentic credentials. Upon arrival, be sure to raise your eyes towards the rich red ceiling and its beautifully ornate golden fixtures. Admire too the much cluttered wall space, where Ireland's many famous sons and daughters are celebrated in dozens of framed photographic shrines. Joyce, Shaw, Beckett and Yeats are just a few of the luminaries comfortably seated within square-bordered frames, and I observed these and more as I sat with my back to Kentish Town Road.

Musing in silence, I tried to imagine the reaction of the punters if one of the greats from the wall were to enter the bar just then. After some thought, I concluded that we the patrons would offer forth restraint in such an event, avoiding any excitable celebrity worshipping that is sadly so much a part of our society today. A few pats on the back would be considered appropriate, and perhaps some kind words, a few well-placed hearty handshakes, and a never-ending fountain of complimentary drinks. Some kissing of the hand and cheeks would be acceptable within reason, modest bowing might be tolerated, and I saw no harm in the hero in question being raised aloft on our shoulders amidst whistles and cheers, if their partial consent was forthcoming.

Turning towards the window, secretly hoping to see Foster & Allen being helped out of a very long white car, my gaze drifted instead towards George's Barbershop, which was positioned directly across the high street. The portrait photos in its window were framed beneath a faded red canopy, and it was immaculate grooming that had ensured their subjects' fame over any claims to music, politics or verse. The good-natured bar patrons didn't appear to notice as I left my half-finished pint on the window mantelpiece, and when George greeted me soon after, welcoming me like a highly valued member of the community, he lost no time in directing me towards a swivelling silver chair. His eyes remained fixed upon the reflective mirror surface as his fingers ran through my hair-do, and when I requested an Oscar Wilde special, his fingers slowly withdrew and his eyes appeared to widen slightly. I attempted to outline the 19th century intellectual bohemian cut as he sprayed my head with water from a clear plastic container, and shaking his head slightly, he began working his silver scissors of greatness until the floor beneath my feet had become a carpet of me.

George was a barber to the stars, and I showed my respect by paying the good man a handsome fee, including a generous tip for the flower I took from his vase and added to my lapel. After navigating the busy traffic outside, I stood nonchalantly inside the corner doors of O'Reilly's and bellowed, "WORK IS THE CURSE OF THE DRINKING CLASSES!"

Heads turned and a few half-smiles briefly emerged before the patrons returned to their drinks and conversations.

My half-finished pint had disappeared from its window-side bench, so I strolled up to the bar and ordered a new one, winking at the barmaid and raising my eyebrows to the picture of me on the wall behind her. While awaiting my free drink, I noticed a handsome fellow standing by himself at the end of the bar. "I SAY GOOD MAN, ARE YOU UP FOR A BIT OF THE OLD FUN STUFF?" Full of brazen confidence, I awaited his retort, noting his incredulous look and the highlighting of his prominent cheekbones. What I need, I thought, is an ivory-topped cane.

Just then, the barmaid placed my drink in front of me and politely demanded a minor fee. Booming with laughter, I replied, "I'M SURE THAT'LL BE FINE." Wandering over to the handsome gent with full pint in hand, I put my arm around his shoulder and whispered in his ear, "I HAVE A VELVET COUCH, YOU KNOW." Minutes later I was lying in the gutter. But I was looking at the stars.

Pembroke Castle

150 Gloucester Avenue NW1 8JA
Nearest tube – Chalk Farm

When the glorious English sun caresses your face like a hot bacon balaclava, grab a drink and sit yourself on the Pembroke Castle's delightful wooden decking. Of course, if it's winter, and the air is full of ice-hardened sleet, don't even think about sitting outside on the patio, because you'll catch your death, good friend. Instead, stay dry and snug on the raised floor area inside.

It was chucking it down on the afternoon I visited Primrose Hill, and my jacket and hat continued to drip on the floor after I'd hung them on the back of my chair. I sat behind a square wooden table in the corner of the raised floor section, and from here I looked around the bar and stroked my bushy sideburns. A small and pretty fireplace crouched in the opposite corner to my right, and high on the wall above this hung a lovely, gilt-edged mirror. Thinking I should inspect my sideburns, I procured a padded seat to stand on.

GOOD LORD! They had become very bushy indeed, as if a head of hair from a Siamese twin had emerged through my very face. I licked my palm in an attempt to dampen them down, and as I did, an evil old woman's face appeared in the mirror.

GOOD LORD! I leapt back, nearly toppling off the chair in surprise. Regarding me sourly, the old woman announced: "WARM MILK, THAT'S WHAT YOU ARE. WARM MILK AND FEATHERS." I spluttered back in protest, raising myself higher upon my tip-toes on the padded wooden seat, one sideburn dry and unruly, the other slightly compressed with my own saliva. Ignoring my attempts at an outburst, she continued: "YOU COULD NEVER DRINK 19 PINTS OF REAL ALE IN 10 MINUTES. NEVER." My eyes crossed slightly in confusion and fear and rage, and I leapt down onto the wooden floorboards and stormed off towards the serving area.

The barwoman seemed somehow suspicious as I requested my family-sized order, but placing a library card on the bar for payment security, I set off with my large, heavy tray. A black mantelpiece ran above the fireplace and I lined most of the pints up along this, placing the subsequent brim-filled glasses upon a square wooden table behind. Nineteen pints = 11,400mls of ale, and most of my first few drinks ended up down the front of my grey jersey because I was basically just pouring them all over my face. By pint number four, time was swiftly ticking by and I found I had the urge to go to the toilet, which was clearly a real nuisance given my tight schedule.

The Gents in the Pembroke Castle are at the bottom of a central staircase, and I took the steps two at a time in order to give myself a fighting chance at very real success. I'd accomplished a quick pit stop and was set to race back upstairs when I suddenly remembered my hands. I HAD TO WASH MY HANDS! The flowing soap dispensed quickly, but the new-fangled push-down taps cut off the water before I'd properly cleansed and removed the soapy residue! CURSES! It took three pushes of the confounded taps until I'd washed my hands satisfactorily and could move towards the automatic hand dryer, which started off really slowly. "YOU TEST ME, HAND DRYER!" I shouted, wiping my hands upon trousers that were already drenched due to my grey jersey literally dripping like a woollen shower curtain. Fortunately, my sideburns were now slicked back with ale, and this gave me an added boost of confidence, but I had to hurry!

I suppose I must have looked like a glistening, sideburned ferret as I emerged from the stairwell, and everyone was staring at me in silence when, to be honest, I really could have used a few hearty cheers. I decided to pump myself up by clapping my own hands as I ran across the bar, knowing I had only 110 seconds to drink 15 pints of real ale. The wicked old woman in the mirror continued to mock me as two pints quickly descended upon my face leaving me with 20 seconds to drink 13 full pints or 7.8 litres of well-poured ale by friendly staff. I was going to do it! Loudly humming Wagner's 'Ride of the Valkyries,' I began chucking it back in triumphant fashion, but just then I was pulled off the padded wooden chair by two uniformed police constables who continued to carry me right off the raised bar area with my wet shoes kicking at empty air.

None of the bar patrons applauded my spirited efforts as I was helped out through the main doors, but sometimes a silent bar can say everything, and I definitely look forward to catching up with them all again for a good natured arm wrestle, but not for money.

Swimmer at the Grafton Arms

13 Eburne Road N7 6AR
Nearest tube – Archway/Holloway Road

Bob Thomas was the Swimmer at the Grafton Arms, and he'd achieved his fame in chlorine waters, despite a bushy moustache that must have added drag to his otherwise eel-like aquatic movements.

It was a chilly winter's afternoon when I made my approach along Eburne Road, and I noticed a swimmer (later revealed as Bob) who had been replicated numerous times on the illustrated pub sign outside. Surrounding the bar exterior however, was a large black tarpaulin-like structure that appeared to cordon the building off from an extra terrestrial that had been discovered inside and was now under strict quarantine. But unrestrained by officials in masks and bright boiler suits who may have been attempting to fumigate the bar, I instead wandered freely beneath the large canopy and past bench tables that were being insularly heated by metal devices far taller than I.

Once inside the bar itself, I strode across to the servery in the most aerodynamic way possible, offering forth the exact change for my pint of real ale; change that might once have been tossed into the deep end depths of a public swimming pool before being retrieved from the bottom by a strong swimmer such as Bob. A small glass cabinet near my wooden bench pew housed various newspaper clippings and photographs of Robert Thomas' aquatic accomplishments, and a pair of well-earned medals were preserved inside as well.

If I hadn't urged my mother to write so many sick notes on pool days I thought, I could have persevered with my lessons and emerged at the other end with damp, matted-down hair and a pub named after me where I could drink like a fish or a swirling piece of thirsty coral. But I was never very good at swimming, and at school the other boys actually used to twirl their wet towels and flick them at me in the changing room. Then they'd tease me about the fact that I still used a flutter-board while they were confidently swimming lengths. Also, my quiet nature and thin rake of a white pasty body disturbed them somehow, and this is why I really had to take my hat off to Bob. He'd absolutely triumphed where I for the most part had failed.

Looking towards his commemorative cabinet, as if through misted up plastic swimming goggles, I raised my glass and whispered, "HERE'S TO YOU, CHIEF. HERE'S TO YOUR EXCEPTIONALLY LARGE FEET WITH RIGID OUTSTRETCHED TOES, AND TO ALL THE MANY BEACH TOWELS YOU HAVE DAMPENED." I consumed a few more pints of most delicious ale, tempted at times to drown my sorrows in the pools of condensation from each clean glass. But first I felt a wee to be in order, so I made my way through the bar towards the toilets, hoping to sit upon the same plastic seat as Bob, even though my need to dispense clear urine could have been easily met from a standing up position. Emerging a short time after, my attention was suddenly taken by a large stuffed otter in a glass case mounted on the wall.

It was baring its teeth and possibly laughing or singing as it stood on a log of sorts, and some grass shoots and little plants were nestled around its enclosure to make it feel more at home in a pub full of carbonated alcoholic liquids. I stood there for a time peering up at the dead little critter in his public house mausoleum, and as I did I saw a tear well up in its eye. It welled and it welled, until eventually it burst, silently descending down facial hair that effortlessly merged into hair of the chest. Staring for answers in its angry/laughing face, it was then that I saw the otter's mouth move. Its little furry lips began moving, and as they did, so too did the rest of its body, and it began gently swaying all the way down to its hairy webbed feet. Shuffling closer, I cocked my ear and attempted to make sense of the tune the otter appeared to be singing. It was 'Many Rivers To Cross.'

"HEY!" I cried out. "HEY EVERYONE! THE OTTER IS ACTUALLY SINGING!"The other patrons looked at each other sceptically, as did the bar staff at first, but gradually they all wandered over, even the chef from the open kitchen who was wiping his hands on his stripy trousers. The otter had become still and silent at that point, but as they all crowded around its cabinet I told them how I'd seen his lips move and how he had swayed rhythmically and was singing 'Many Rivers To Cross' and how a tear had fallen from his sad looking otter's face. The entire bar appeared spellbound by this and they all stood riveted and transfixed and pointing, waiting and hoping to see it happen again. They waited and waited and waited and waited until eventually those on the outer edge of the crowd heard me jimmy open Bob's commemorative cabinet at the opposite end of the bar and they turned to see me reaching inside to grab his medals.

The white bonnet of the police car was quite hot, and as my hands extended in a spread-eagled fashion across it, a large, genuine tear ran down my furry, unshaven face, causing a slight sizzling sound when it made contact with the racy, engine-charged bonnet.

South

Amersham Arms

388 New Cross Road SE14 6TY
Nearest tube – New Cross

The New Cross area is well populated with students from Goldsmiths College, but the afternoon crowd in the Amersham Arms is also made up of some good-natured and sensible older folk.

A collection of welcoming Irish gents were gathered around the servery when I completed a modest arrival, and they politely allowed me access to the counter where I placed an order for a lovely pint of ale.

Behind the U-shaped bar were various cups and trophies, including an old sewing machine, awarded, I assumed, for Best Embroidered Handkerchief. Affixed to the ceiling were small cartwheel light fittings, and alongside these flew spread-eagled football jerseys in tight, geese-like formation. Directly opposite my upholstered burgundy seat was a slightly raised area for live music events, and drummers would have to be mindful of their bottoms, I thought, given the small fireplace to the rear of the stage. Double-decker buses paused occasionally outside the windows to my left, and many of the upstairs passengers looked in at me as if I was undressing in a well-lit room at night, when in fact I was simply retrieving soft blue fluff from my bellybutton and adding it to the collection I'd amassed within an old Vegemite jar.

On the shelf behind me lay a row of interesting and somewhat weathered books. I flicked through a particular work from Catherine Cookson and was surprised to see a small slip of folded paper fall from within its pages onto my lap. Curious, I unfolded the neatly pressed note, revealing a handwritten message written in block capitals that read: DEFUSE THE EXPLOSIVES! Looking nervously about me, I began urgently refolding the note many times over before slipping it in my mouth, together with a large gulp of traditional ale.

My eyes were drowning when I noticed an exposed ventilation shaft that ran in an 'L' shape along the ceiling above the servery. It had been painted a fairly innocuous chocolate brown colour and was slightly hidden from view by a ceiling support post. AHA! The tightly packed explosives were harboured within its very bowels! Glancing around the bar at the good-natured old gents, each as harmless as puff pie pastry, I began to imagine them all as molten, burnt out corpses. There was no time to lose. I had to hurry.

"TELL MY WIFE I LOVE HER!" I screamed at the lovely older barwoman, and she looked at me with a sincere expression of concern as I sprinted across the wooden floorboards with robotic swinging arms towards the STAFF ONLY door to the right of the bar. Gasping for breath at the top of the stairs, I soon discovered that the entrance to the ventilation shaft was narrower than the ones I had remembered from the movies but I sucked in my guts and thighs and squirmed on through, all thoughts focused on reaching the fuse-box in time. After thrusting along a mere matter of yards however, I found myself well and truly stuffed, arms pinned at the sides. I couldn't budge in either direction. An ever-decreasing clock flashed through my mind. TWO FOUR SIX ZERO ONE NINE THREE SEVEN!

Just then I noticed a rectangular vent at the bottom of the shaft with a small open grille that faced down into the bar. I contorted my face towards it and started pleading to the staff and patrons below. I pleaded like a goat stuck down a ravine, but perhaps at a slightly higher, more manic pitch. The previously pleasant banter from the bar quickly dried up like a drip of soapy tap water beneath a savage gust of hand-dryer air, and all eyes looked skyward to my desperate chequered face.

I must have lost a good 400 calories when my rescuer fired up the blowtorch an hour or so later, and it was as if I was swimming in the very ale that I had so recently been served up and consumed. The policeman remained rather stony-faced as he escorted my drenched person off the premises, and I tried to warn him about the explosives, but he wasn't in the least bit interested, and simply jerked harder on my handcuffs.

Crown & Greyhound

73 Dulwich Village SE21 7BJ
Nearest tube – North Dulwich rail

Built in the late 19th century, the Crown & Greyhound is a large and impressive slice of preserved Victoriana, quietly imposing standards and traditions in the heart of Dulwich Village. Original fittings have been retained and respectfully maintained within, and one can still imagine frail old men being rolled for fun inside butter churns on the wide promenade outside.

Partitions divide the front of the bar into three main sections, and a segregated smoke-free area to the right provides a solemn and dignified environment to read a newspaper or to write furious ranting letters to the editor of said newspaper. Sealing myself into this fresher side-room setting with ale, I discovered an exquisite collection of wooden settles, including a particularly intricate piece with dog heads carved onto its armrest ends. It's worth noting too the swivelling glass panels on the partition wall that resemble great artefacts of a previous civilization, and the elaborate plaster design on the marzipan beams and ceiling, which is of a Tutankhamun style.

If Dulwich Village were suddenly to be buried under a huge multitude of ash and lava I laughed, historians unearthing this miraculously intact room 1000 years from now would clearly believe that I had been laid to rest amongst ornate funereal offerings and sacrificial effigies. The tile designs around the dormant fireplace for instance, and the cushion covers with their embroidered motifs and topographical reference points could all be construed as symbols of ritual corpse burnings. And the emblem of harvest evoked by the flowery pub carpet patterns hinted, I thought, at an alignment of the sun with the crops, and my rebirth after death as a prince.

A Rikki Lee-Jones tune was being broadcast through plastic, wall-mounted speakers, causing me to question its appropriateness as the musical piece for my fast approaching death rattle. But there was little time to dwell on such matters, and I began to prepare instead for the enveloping crush of hot, pressed ash. It was important that my preserved corpse wasn't unearthed, poised as it was, in readiness for a trip to the bar, so I began eyeing up the nearby dog head settle as a suitable open casket.

Lying horizontally along the length of its green cushioned bench seat, I wiped fresh ale residue from my mouth before gently clasping my hands together upon my breast. Decorative guards faced inwards from the settle's wooden backing, and the ever-loyal dog heads stayed vigilantly on duty at each end of their master. I lay perfectly still (with the exception of my restless, window-wiper feet), while silently drifting incense smoke was replaced with the sound of bar talk, laughter, and unpreserved jaws munching through salted potato crisps. Feeling at peace with myself, I slowly drifted away into a very deep sleep.

I must have slept for a good 400 years before I was awoken with a start by a middle-aged man who shook me on the shoulder. Behind him was a woman of similar age who also regarded me with concern. It took me a moment or two to work out where I was before I suddenly became enlightened with my god-like status and leapt up, ordering the dogs to "MURDER THE BASTARD GRAVE ROBBERS."

I was chanting/shouting as I ran through the main bar area, throwing patterned cushions about like feather-downed ninja stars, and when I reached the central bar partition, I raised my arms to the heavens before disappearing in a cloud of smoke.

Eagle

231 Battersea Park Road SW11 4LG
Nearest tube – Queenstown Road

Congealed custard had accumulated on my unshaven chin when I eventually emerged from the Eagle pub, and it tasted like your mother's homemade custard special, except it was obviously just so much better.

My visit had begun at a seat near the door, where my pint of ale had rested upon a chessboard that was engrained into the wooden table surface. Divider windows to my left appeared to have been slashed by the blade of a passing highwayman, and behind me were rows of empty champagne bottles, each one personalised with hand-written messages. A fair crowd had turned up to watch a rugby match on a large flimsy screen, but because my view of the game was obscured, I instead imagined a team of squirrels playing a team of field mice with a rugby ball made from a somewhat weathered acorn.

The opposite wall was dominated by an unusual half moon stretch of wooden panels, upon which shelves of books resided beside a central wood-framed mirror. Above the mirror sat an impressive looking golden sports trophy, and curious to read its engraved inscription, I picked up my pint glass and strode across for a better look. It was slightly out of my reach, and so I clambered onto a bar stool and stretched out with grasping fingers.

"OI, DON'T YOU TOUCH THAT!" bellowed the good-natured barman from behind the servery, briefly drowning out the roar of the televised match, but I had already yanked on the prize, levering the trophy down like the barman himself would pull a pint of very fine ale. There was a slight whirring sound, and the entire half-circular wall area suddenly began swivelling around, along with the fireplace beneath and the stool upon which I stood. It was like one of those haunted house secret passage moments, and I caught a glimpse of the barman's anguished face and the bewildered expressions of the patrons within the bar, as the half moon wall and I slowly rotated in a horizontal manner before completing our turn and stopping with a juddering halt.

Finding myself on the other side of the wall in fire-lit darkness, still clutching the sports trophy and my pint of tasty ale, I observed that I was in a damp and rather musty cavern. There was a deathly silence apart from the crackle of burning wood from the fire, and as my eyes began to adjust to the gloom, I noted some stalactites hanging from the ceiling, and a perfectly circular hole within a nearby limestone wall. A bat flapped by as I climbed down off my bar stool and meandered across the wet stony floor towards the wall hole, which reminded me of a window in the Flintstones' house.

Peering through it, I could make out the origins of a wet and slimy tunnel, while in the distance my ears pricked up at the sound of automatic gunfire. I'd only dropped by the Eagle for a few quick ales, but after hoisting myself over the base of the circular ledge, I soon found myself sliding at a furious pace down a natural limestone hydro-slide, desperately trying not to spill ale through my hair around the twisty corners.

Eventually I landed in some foam casing that was clearly being used for the purpose of packing large weaponry inside shipping crates. It was some kind of underground ammunitions factory, and the sound of discharging shells reverberating off the limestone walls was very noisy. So acknowledging the friendly wave of an elderly Oriental man, I walked towards his small wooden boat, which was moored alongside a simple jetty on a very narrow underground river.

I accepted his offer of a sightseeing cruise, and as we drifted downstream, he pointed out a side cavern where large rubies were being mined by heavy digging machinery. When I questioned him about the thick yellow nature of the gently flowing river water, he laughed: "THAT'S WHERE CUSTARD COMES FROM!" I leaned out of the old wooden boat and stuck my face right in, finding it warm, gooey and most deliciously tasty. After four hours had passed, he dropped me at the base of a steep set of solid rock stairs, motioning for me to ascend them, so I shook his hand heartily and stepped out of his quaint wooden vessel. I climbed for some distance, reminded of the boarded off escalators in the London Underground where the only thing UNDER CONSTRUCTION is lies.

A distant light beckoned, and I was as surprised as the next man when I emerged through an open trapdoor behind the bar in the Eagle pub. The barman shook his head, and motioned towards the yellow mess around my face. Blushing through the custard like an oven-fresh raspberry scone, I shuffled my shoes along the traditional red-patterned pub carpet, generating no electricity on my way to the door. Turning briefly to face the quiet, staring patrons, I then departed with my tail between my legs, and it was more of a long spindly field mouse tail than a bushy squirrel equivalent.

Effra

38A Kellet Road SW2 1EB
Nearest tube – Brixton

The Effra pub is an eight-minute walk from Brixton Underground, but if you run very fast you can cover the distance in a speedy one minute and seven seconds.

Two separate entrance doors face onto Kellet Road from the pub itself, and if you're looking to shave mere milliseconds off your time, enter the first one. Inside to the right, a bright red booth surrounds a wall-mounted telephone like a large, ill-fitting motorbike helmet. To the left, a central serving area caters for two separate bars, and the afternoon I dropped by the staff member on duty was working between the two like a submarine engine room attendant, darting here and there pulling levers and plugging holes. I placed my well-poured ale upon a small round table that was shedding varnish like skin, as if it had recently returned from a bar table package tour to Acapulco. Jerk Chicken was advertised as a Special on a blackboard alongside this, reminding me of the many names I had been called in my formative years, including "JERK", "CHICKEN", and "SPECIAL". But a bright and cheerful reggae track kept my mood perky, and I cheered myself on by smiling broadly and drinking faster.

I was approaching the servery for another pint with my hand outstretched in readiness, when all of a sudden the reggae track began skipping, and

I found myself frozen and rigid to the spot. I couldn't move a muscle, captured in a wild-eyed, glass-wielding pose, like some future Madame Tussauds' wax figure of me. The music continued its uh, uh, uh, uh, uh, uh, uh assault, and through round unblinking eyes, I watched the barmaid duck into the office behind the bar. I continued to stare at the horizontal mirror strips on the office door, and when

The next thing I knew I was seated back behind my table and the pint of ale I had been about to purchase was already two thirds empty. I was thoroughly confused. My fingers pawed gently at my scalp, and when I removed my hand, I saw that dandruff had pasted beneath my nails like white sand. Glancing around at my surroundings, I noticed people sitting at tables nearby who hadn't been there when I'd ventured to the bar only moments before, and when I caught their staring eyes, they immediately looked away. A completely different reggae track was now bouncing buoyantly along, and I checked the rim of my glass for evidence of unusual saliva or traces of another's mucky gums. Instead I simply found my own slug-like remnants, and the familiar faint scent of birdseed. What on earth had happened? Had I missed something? But how?

I was raising a fresh pint towards my lips in a tilting manner, observing the thick, bread knife-applied nicotine on the ceiling, when suddenly the song began skipping again. Uh, uh, uh, uh, uh, uh, uh, uh, uh, uh, uh, uh, uh, uh, uh. I sat frozen, hunched rigid in my chair, and as the

I was now seated at a different table across in the opposite bar. It had a black Formica top, upon which were four full pints of ale and three empty pint glasses. My jacket was loosely draped over the back of my new chair, and my black pub review diary lay dishevelled upon the floor with some of its loose contents (including pressed leaves and waterproof bandages), now rudely scattered in disarray. It was all very mysterious, this sudden jumping around the bar, and I picked up the first of the four full pints and took a large gulp.

Looking around at my new surroundings, I noticed curtains that were tied back like loose ponytails, their designs resembling expensive golden gift-wrapping paper. Older men were slapping domino pieces upon a small square table, and glass lampshades were the colour of shells and resembled women's hairstyles that have been

I found myself standing in the toilets, my hands extended out beneath the blasting gust of the silver hand-dryer vent. My hands were very red and very hot. When I re-entered the bar area, everything was enshrouded in darkness, and there were no customers and no members of staff. I tried both entrance doors, but they were both securely fastened. I was locked inside the Effra pub, so I walked through the lift-up door in the servery and helped myself to a drink. All was silent.

The next morning I was awoken by a cleaner who found me asleep behind the bar, my head propped up by a pile of crisp packets that were heaped in a mound upon the floor. Still half asleep, my mind awash with thoughts of sword-fighting and butter, I panicked, immediately leaping over the bar counter where I began running towards the large red telephone booth motorbike helmet shouting, "YOU CAN'T HURT ME."

Half Moon

10 Half Moon Lane SE24 9HU
Nearest tube – Herne Hill rail

The Half Moon is a splendid old Victorian alehouse, dating back to around 1895, and not too many years ago it also served as a venue for some of Britain's most famous bands. Today it remains a prominent landmark in Herne Hill, and as I was approaching its broad, majestic frontage, I observed two silhouetted figures in a first floor window who were punching each other in the face.

If you're partial to a bit of the old fisticuffs yourself, make your way up to the boxing gym, which is housed above the pub. Arts and crafts enthusiasts should remain below however, in order to appreciate the Half Moon's impressive and beautifully preserved back-painted mirror collection. These mirrors are a real treasure for any pub, and you can find them in a cosy rear snug at the far end of the Public Bar. Each piece is decorated with a colourful array of flowers and plant life, and swans, sparrows and herons have also been intricately applied by hand onto the back of the glass. As I looked around the snug, I noticed that nature in its many forms was actually a dominating theme of the surroundings. The traditional pub carpet featured flowers, leaves and stems, as did the furnished designs of four upholstered chairs. Six glass dividers paid a white-etched homage to greenery, and even the woodcarvings around each back-painted mirror featured a particular variety of fern.

I was sitting quietly, noting all this nature (and the smiling and attentive staff), when I suddenly felt a peculiar movement upon my left shoe. Looking down, I noticed that my lace was loose and untied. Given the unique and particularly complex system of knots and bows I use for securing my laces, this was a most unusual incident. In fact, the very thought that this intricate network of loops had been breached caused me, at that moment, to loudly dry-retch. The colour drained from my face and I began panicking, worried that my foot had grown into some sort of 'huge foot', thus causing my shoe to expand and the lace to miraculously unthread. Removing my shoe, I discovered however that my sock-enshrouded toes and sole were thankfully still at a sensible size and length, and so whistling loudly, I confidently retied the lace, dismissing the whole incident as nothing more than some stupid sick joke.

Above me in the rear snug was an elaborate mock chandelier, its features including fake candle bulbs and six little pissing boy characters who appeared to be riding jet skis. The whole fitting swayed ever so slightly when the outside door to the Public Bar was opened, and when I looked down again, I saw that both of my shoelaces were now untied, their four ends splayed out on the carpet like drunken worms. Grimacing slightly, I set about retying the pair of them, adding some extra tight bows to each. Then, placing my elbows on my knees and my hands on my face, I stared like a wooden Balinese mask at the fist-like gnarled knots of white lace below. I was staring like this, with burning eyes, when the flowery pub carpet suddenly came to life.

Rising out of the thick textured design, wavering about like a cartoon snake, came forth a spindly plant stem made from dyed woollen fibres, and I watched open-mouthed as it burrowed between the dense, tightly packed folds of my left shoelace. Glimpsing further movement upon the floor, I was horrified to discover that the precious contents of my brown satchel were now strewn all about the place, and threaded leaves and petals from the carpet pattern had begun wreaking havoc with my personal things. The entire floor was just going nuts, and it reminded me of some sped-up nature documentary about growth, renewal and horticulture in pubs.

I immediately leapt to my feet and began stamping down with hard kicking leg movements upon the vile grasping greenery that threatened from every side. The carpet was soon entangling my ankles however, so struggling free, I clambered up onto one of the upholstered chairs. But the stems on the very seat fabric itself began clutching at my shins, slithering up my hairy legs and snaring the daggy parts of my well-worn trousers. I leapt down onto some of the larger plants, hoping to squish them with the full force of my body weight, and after smashing my glass upon the lip of a small wooden table, I used its jagged edge to sever more of the beasts. I was throwing solid glass ashtrays at the floor to cull the emerging forest when the grip of vines around my legs began to tighten. Attempting to make a run for the Public Bar, I tripped and knocked myself out on the side of the radiator.

Beautiful swans and herons were drifting around my head when I awoke to find two men wearing boxing gloves looking worriedly at the condensed mass of tiny, hand-written scribbles in my pub review diary. Beside them, a member of staff mopped at the damp carpet and picked up shards of broken glass.

Hand in Hand

7 Crooked Billet SW19 4RQ
Nearest tube – Wimbledon tube/rail

It's not everyday that one leaves a pub with grass stains on their bottom, but my advice is to leave your white trousers at home when you head for the Hand in Hand in Wimbledon.

It was a fine summer's afternoon when I descended upon the Crooked Billet area, home to the fine pub in question, and this followed a quick and pleasant walk from the famous Common nearby. Birds were chirping, leaves they rustled, and white pasty legs were frying like lengths of pita bread upon the sizeable patch of grassy agriculture that lay directly opposite the pub itself. It was outside on this gentle lush field that many of the Hand's customers had congregated to enjoy the sun's glorious rays, and I observed them drinking alcoholic beverages like thirsty plants, watering themselves in order to prevent a slow and parched death.

Ducking inside the low-ceilinged cottage pub, I was carefully administered a pint of tasty ale within a plastic glass before I set off across the road to lay claim to my very own plot of turf. I was fortunate enough to find a tree I could lean my back upon, and the pre-flattened grass beside it appeared to have been pressed by a pair of very obese buttocks indeed. It was exciting to think that Andre the Giant had been sitting there mere moments before, and the grass did seem warm in fact, and actually rather sweaty. I sat and surveyed the lush outdoor scene like a little fluffy rabbit with bright eyes burning like fire and a coat smelling of singed fur. The scene itself was a bit like the Glastonbury music festival, except there was no stage, no music, and no weird people drenched in their own urine and others.

After lofting a contented sigh into the wayward breeze, I noticed a splattering of empty plastic pint glasses nearby. These protruded out of the long grass like glass tulips, and before long an efficient and zestful barmaid came around to pile them up into a Pisa Tower type structure. She was already on her way back across the road to the pub however, when I noticed that she had missed one of her charges. I decided that I would see to its safe return myself, and as I stared at its plastic material with glassy eyes, I was sure I saw it move slightly.

I was very certain indeed in fact that the plastic glass had moved slightly by itself. I quickly came to the conclusion that a mole had its ear against the earth beneath and was using the glass to listen in like a spy to what was being said and done in our civilised outside world, dictating everything to another mole who was typing it all into a computer and saving the information in a file named: BURY THE HUMANS IN THE DIRT WE'VE POOED IN.

My bottom was getting sore at this point, so I stood up, noting my own small round prints in the grass, and then I ever so delicately wandered across to the solitary plastic glass. Very quietly, I crouched down beside it and whispered: "YOU MOLES ARE DUE FOR DEATH BY MY HAND." I leaned back slightly, eyes and ears peeled for some sort of reaction or the sudden clatter of keyboards being struck by dirty paws. Nothing. They were sitting tight, playing the waiting game with me, clearly paranoid beyond belief that I had unearthed their sheet-metal enforced, wall-lined underground laboratory. I had to act fast now before they informed the others. The world's oil resources! Of course! Those mole bastards were masterminding a mass burrow into the earth to seize control of the world's oil fields in order to cripple motorists and redistribute small pockets of huge multi-national wealth amongst billions of filthy, dirty moles!

I seized their plastic glass sound amplifier and immediately began burrowing into the earth myself. Using the former drinking vessel in a shovel-like manner, I scooped the grass and topsoil away, hoisting it randomly over my shoulder. The moles were centimetres away, I thought, they had to be, but after furiously removing a good foot of muddy dirt, I had uncovered nothing. So I simply dug faster. A small family group behind me were receiving a veritable shower of mud and worms upon their tidy hairstyles and pleasant natures, but better a little dirt and soil rain on their picnic I thought, than watch future generations of their well-polished family growing up blind with large hairy, muddy snouts.

My hole in the grassy patch meanwhile, had at this point become what I would define as 'gaping,' and still not a trace of fur or sophisticated satellite navigational equipment. My frustration became channelled via robotic-like arm digging actions, and was sprinkled with shouted utterings, including: "DIE! DIE! DIE! DIE! DIE! DIE! I'LL KILL YOU ALL!!"

It was hot work under that very fine English sun, and in a way I was pleased when the police officers arrived to relieve me of my shift. I expressed my gratitude wholeheartedly, although I did make the point that they probably should have brought some superior digging equipment with them, such as those funny looking mini-bulldozer things that jerk about like robotic teapots.

Hermit's Cave

28 Camberwell Church Street SE5 8QU
Nearest tube – Denmark Hill rail

Despite its name, this lively Camberwell tavern promotes a congenial atmosphere of friendly chatter and cosy pub charm, and once you've entered through the Saloon Bar entrance, you'll step on sturdy wooden floorboards, rather than damp, limestone rocks or the splintered bones of an antelope carcass.

Various knick-knacks and treasure pieces greet you high above the bar, including a somewhat weathered mannequin's head, porcelain jars, and other such items that befit an era of good old-fashioned style. On tiered shelving beneath are many very clean glasses, all lined up shoulder to shoulder, and you can almost imagine them shuffling along a factory assembly line, ready to be dropped into a mincer and turned into shard sausages. I collected my pint of ale and walked around to the left-hand side of the bar, settling into a faded old green couch that backed onto the window.

A blackboard was mounted above the central partition doorway to my right, and someone had quizzically written on it: IF WE DIDN'T LET YOU WIN EVERY NOW AND THEN YOU WOULD LOSE HEART. To my left, a mirror in an elaborate wooden frame hung gracefully above a fireplace, and in front of this, suspended from the ceiling by four small chains and hooks was a metallic, cylindrical tube with rounded black ends.

It was hanging very high out of reach, and I tried to work out what in the blazes it was for as I made my way towards a white-frosted door that was set in the opposite wall. Pausing at the entrance to the toilets, I observed a lovely framed picture of some flowers set against a black background, and on closer examination I saw a pair of cheeky birds hidden near the bottom of the image, one of which was tucking into a grape. As I spent a penny, I began to think about hidden things. Hidden birds, hidden meanings, hidden talent, hidden money, hidden treasure. I made sure to wash my hands thoroughly and dried them.

Back at my couch seat, I once again looked up towards the ceiling-suspended metallic tube, this time picturing its contents. Inside I saw a rolled treasure map that was quilled with fading ink, ribboned with antelope hair, and awaiting retrieval from its dusty tomb. My fellow patrons were reading newspapers and talking softly as I began scaling the perimeter of the fireplace beneath the elaborately framed mirror.

Various leaflets denoting local activities had been neatly piled on the ledge of the fire, but these were dispensed to the floor by my clumsy feet, and the pane of mirror glass shook with fear as I grappled with its wooden supports. As the other patrons began observing my progress, I became anxious to reach the treasure map before they worked out the clues and became poisoned with thoughts of greed and thievery. Pointing towards the sports pages of their papers, I screamed, "LOOK, LOOK!" But they remained somehow captivated by the fact that I was desperately clinging to the side of the pub wall, and so to divert their attention, I turned and leapt into the air like a springing monkey, curling my hairy, grasping fingers around the upper rim of the mysterious metallic tube.

My outstretched legs were firm and rigid as I silently swung like an East European trapeze artist in the rafts of a travelling show. Accumulated dust transferred itself onto my fingers, and I was wondering if this included the flakes of another's skin as ceiling plaster began falling onto my head and protruding nose. With the treasure map nearly within my grasp, the crowd below looked up with a keener interest, and so I barked out, "READ YOUR PRECIOUS FOOTBALL RESULTS, YOU LEECHES! THE TREASURE IS MINE! IT'S MINE! IT'S MINE! IT'S MINE! IT'S MINE! IT'S MINE! IT'S MINE!" The first of the four hooks became dislodged from the ceiling at this point, closely followed by its counterpart alongside, and I slid down the now vertical cylinder, clutching desperately to its rounded end. Ceiling plaster was showering down, and just as the final screws gave way, I saw my reflection adorned upon the adjacent wall mirror, thinking it resembled an ancient cave drawing of a primitive man with a dough ball head covered in sprinkles of grated coconut.

King's Head

84 Upper Tooting Road SW17 7PB
Nearest tube – Tooting Bec

My head was held snugly beneath my arm as I reflected upon the historic decorative features in the King's Head pub, where the exquisite wall tiles near the Gents were of particular interest, together with the divider windows and their original etched glass engravings.

The cavernous Victorian interior greets one like a welcome handshake from a fellow hand that has first been wiped clean on a smart pair of trousers, and after placing my smiling head on the bar top, I swivelled it about for a look at what was on offer. Various sets of keys hung from hooks on the elaborately carved central bar, and I imagined looking through the keyholes of these, spying upon very ordinary domestic scenes, apart from in one room where an adult male was to be found wrestling a snake-like woollen draught stopper. After selecting my choice of ale with a pointing finger, I proceeded with laden hands through a doorway at the back, above which hung a sign entitled: LADIES. I'm a man and have no use for sanitary boxes, but it wasn't a female convenience I had entered, but rather a grand rear room, the Ladies in question being hidden away in a far corner.

Carelessly forgetting I'd removed my head, I began pouring cold wet ale down the front of my clean and pressed shirt. The staff and patrons looked on concerned, so waving out to console them, I juggled my head from hand to hand as I walked back to the bar for a fresh pint.

Near my wooden bench seat was a pool table crouched on stubbly legs, and I was surprised to see a quick flash of movement at the far end of its plush tabletop. Peering across to the source of this darting flit, I hoped it would present itself further. But all was still as I ran my eyes across the scene like a poised cat awaiting the smallest movement of a foot beneath a blanket. I was carefully tilting my glass towards my lowered head however, when I spied a sudden skittering near the pool table's right middle pocket. Fearing strange forces at play, I wandered across traditional pub carpet to investigate. Setting my pint glass and head upon a narrow wooden ledge, I paused for a minute to admire the attention to detail in the ornately etched glass dividers. But just then, a small chattering noise erupted directly behind me. Spinning my head in a neat 180-degree turn, I found myself confronted with a large white rabbit that was standing rigidly erect within a corner pocket of the pool table.

It stared at me with its pink beady eyes, and its protruding teeth moved in a piston-like way, as if stapling together the pages of a complaints form. Farmers aren't keen on rabbits, due to the fact that they scurry about and multiply and produce very small brown droplet poos on the land. Immediately concerned for the well-preserved surroundings of the historic King's Head pub therefore, I perceived this rabbit before me as a major threat.

Moving ever so cautiously towards the pool table with my hands outstretched in a gesture of strangulation, I quickly made my lunge. But the rabbit darted back within the hole, emerging almost immediately through another pocket at the opposite end of the table. I ran clumsily around towards it, my movements vaguely steered from my shouting head on the ledge. The rabbit submerged with apparent ease however, only to appear yet again from a cushioned middle pocket. I fumbled within my pockets for a £1 coin, dropping it into the sliding metal slot at the side of the table. Shiny cork balls rolled down inner corridors like barrels, and when the rabbit jerked up from an opposing corner, I swung wildly at the beast with a pool cue I had retrieved from a nearby wall rack. The co-ordination between my brain and body proved fruitless however, and my cue end simply struck at the warm pellet breath of the fur-coated pest.

After pouring my pint of ale down the nearest hole, I then began appropriating the drinks of other patrons in an attempt to flush the vermin out. Frothy lager, stout and cider collided and gathered with my ale at the ball collection slot, but the elusive rabbit continued to taunt and jeer from whichever pocket it saw fit. Reverting back to my pool cue, I began smashing it wildly against the six holes of the table, trailing the white rabbit with flying wooden splinters and general whacking behaviour. Having destroyed my first cue, I pried another from the wall rack, but I was at that moment restrained by members of the bar staff.

My head continued to shout from its ledge position, and when the rabbit popped up from the left middle pocket, its mouth was full of £1 coins.

Prince of Wales

38 Old Town SW4 OLB
Nearest tube – Clapham Common

The old town quarter is home to some of Clapham's more interesting pubs, and the Prince of Wales in particular, is well worth a stop. Its homely atmosphere provides a pleasant alternative to the modern High Street bars, and your change is placed on your soap-lathered palm, rather than upon a cold, mortuary-like silver tray.

I arrived early on a weekday afternoon, and finding seats to be plentiful, I sat myself on a marble-red padded bench seat just inside the front entrance door. Two small white dogs shared my long wall seat also, and the largest of the pair seemed keen to bite the likes of me. Deliberately spilling some of my ale in order to mark my territory therefore, I then bulged my eyes out and proceeded to hum a shrill warning at a tone indecipherable to the human ear.

The walls and ceiling in the Prince of Wales are bathed in a similar marble-red shade to the upholstered bench seating, and the numerous wooden chairs and stools are brightly painted in colours such as blue, orange and white. My table was covered by a strange, grey, cocoon-like coating, as if it were soon to emerge as a more beautiful pub table, capable of flight, upturned drinks and smashed glasses. I was imagining myself chasing it through a meadow with a large net and a rifle when

I suddenly remembered that I had to call my local M.P.

Her number was hand-written in biro on a small strip of card that was tucked inside my sock, and retrieving it, I spied a white telephone mounted on the wall beside me. A familiar woman's voice answered, and stating my name, I asked to speak to my M.P. There was a pause before the voice hurriedly announced that I had reached the wrong number and the line went dead. I dialled again and again, certain it was the correct and corresponding number, but despite my numerous attempts, I repeatedly encountered an engaged tone.

It was then, perhaps in frustration, that I pressed the star button, or the * button as it appears in the bottom corner of a telephone's digit pad. As I did, the two dogs immediately began barking, and spinning round, I looked on in horror as a veritable junk shop of dusty old artefacts suddenly began falling with an almighty clatter from the previously barren ceiling. Each piece descended a short distance before hanging, suspended in the air, and it was like watching oxygen masks released inside an aeroplane, except the masks in this case were comprised of things like bird cages, traffic lights and stuffed alligators.

I slowly replaced the handle on the telephone, still watching in disbelief as a yellow Oriental cart with a light blue hairdryer wrapped round its axel gently swayed above the bar area. The other patrons stared towards the heavens with large gaping mouth holes, and the friendly little white dog continued barking lightly while its larger, unfriendly equivalent sat quite still, looking at me without blinking. Feeling like a cat that knows it's close to death, I attempted to find a quiet secluded place, and so coughing politely from the descending dust, I walked with averted gaze past the serving area towards the back of the bar.

Nailed to the wall above the rear toilet door is a tin street sign denoting TROTT STREET SW11, and the door itself is covered in square mirrored panels so you can see yourself full of urine before you pass it. Inside, I headed for the cubicle in the Gents, and after locking the door behind me, I stood bent-over the toilet. ROYAL DOULTON MADE IN ENGLAND was inscribed on the rim of the porcelain, and my eyes lowered further, expecting to see the reflected image of a manic face with small hairs extending from the nostrils. Instead, I found myself looking through an oblong window at blue sky and the tops of swiftly moving clouds.

I stood transfixed above the toilet in the Prince of Wales, my eyes glued to the window at the bottom of the bowl, and looking through it, I noticed I was now descending through the clouds. After emerging out into clear skies beneath, I observed patches of farmed land where the toilet water should have been, and it wasn't long before residential housing announced the outskirts of a large city.

People on London Bridge were pointing up at me in shock as I headed swiftly towards the skyscrapers in Canary Wharf, and the last thing I can remember is a loud burst of air blasting out from the hand-dryer.

Wishing Well Inn

79 Choumert Road SE15 4AR
Nearest tube – Peckham Rye rail

Some may argue that the proliferation of in-bar television coverage has ruined the cosy, intimate feel of the marvellous London pub. Certainly this would seem to be the case from my own experience, and I would hesitate to find favour with an establishment that overtly promotes such base, barbaric behaviour. But the television in the Wishing Well Inn made for quite a welcome change. Here's why.

I was sitting at the far left hand end of the bar, acquainting myself with the wonderful dark wood and etched glass interior, when I noticed a bracket-mounted TV wedged up in the corner beside the servery. It wasn't showing the footy, or the darts, or even lions polishing off the shredded bloody remains of a young gazelle. Instead, the grainy black and white footage simply depicted a static, overhead shot of two pool tables and a single jukebox machine. There was no sound at all, and clearly not much action. After staring riveted for about fifteen minutes, I laughed and turned back to my pub review notebook. 'VERY FRIENDLY STAFF, NICE STURDY BARSTOOLS…'

Soon afterwards, a couple walked through the door behind me from Choumert Road, and I raised my glass in welcome as they quickly disappeared away to the right of the bar. I shrugged and smiled sheepishly, drinking a toast to all the many bar patron strangers who had chosen to avoid eye contact with my happy face. I was about to order myself another pint of delicious ale when I noticed some movement up on the TV screen. Two characters were now walking up to one of the pool tables, and as I gazed more intently, I realised with shock that they were the couple who I'd just seen enter the bar! They were now live on TV!

I dropped my glass with a clatter on the bar top and laughed aloud, pointing to the screen and turning to see if anyone else was aware of this extraordinary turn of events. The barman had moved down to my end of the bar and he was staring at me with his eyebrows slightly raised. An older man sitting at the bar close by was also staring at me. He had his arms folded and his cheeks were tightly sucked in. The couple meanwhile, were now playing pool on the TV, and I refocused my attention on them, completely enthralled. After some time had passed however, I felt restless. Where was this mysterious televised poolroom? How could I get closer to the action? I wanted my own crack at the TV gig! Shutting my book loudly, I winked at the old man before striding off purposefully in the very same footsteps as the couple on the Wishing Well television screen.

At the far end of the bar I encountered a doorway, and instead of proceeding straight ahead to the Gents, I turned left towards a large back room. Inside, the pool tables and the jukebox were almost unrecognisable due to their bright, vibrant colours. But I recognised the famous couple, and they looked at each other, embarrassed, as I waved at them excitedly.

The TV camera, I soon discovered, was hidden behind a round plastic fitting, mounted high in the entranceway corner. After clearing my throat, I paused, awaiting my cue. AND GO. Staring straight down the lens, I began walking slowly towards the camera, my pen raised to my mouth like a microphone as I introduced, in sombre tones, a news report bulletin about a volcano erupting and a catastrophic river of lava. But then, seeing the lava flowing straight towards me from beneath the camera, I turned and fled in horror towards the pool tables, only to dance straight back, Broadway style, kicking my feet up high and singing 'We're In The Money.'

A brief puppet show followed, starring the ends of my bunched up jumper sleeves, and then, moving directly under the camera out of sight, I slowly shimmied up the wall until my face suddenly appeared directly in front of the lens, taking up the full screen. I stared with wild eyes before pretending to actually start eating the camera. I was chewing with big, exaggerated jaw movements when the bartender grabbed my legs and pulled me down.

I found myself outside with my trousers slightly torn. But I was certainly won over by the charms of the Wishing Well Inn, and maybe when I next return I'll pick up that VHS copy I asked for as the door slammed.

West

City Barge

27 Strand-on-the-Green W4 3PH
Nearest tube – Kew Bridge rail/Gunnersbury tube/rail

Many unpleasant wealthy folk pay millions of pounds sterling for the privilege of a decent riverside view, but after parting with a mere £2.67, I relaxed in comfort beside an upstairs window table in the pleasant City Barge pub. Furiously jangling the many spare coins in my left trouser pocket, my eyes were presented with a splendid view of the Thames, unobstructed except for a bothersome tree on the path of the Strand outside and a pane of clear glass in the window itself.

Swans floated past on the river, presumably kicking their feet beneath the water; feet which, perhaps, weren't quite as graceful as their necks and heads. A train clickety-clacked noisily across an old greyish-green bridge to my left, followed swiftly after by another train, and I think this second train was a police train and it was chasing the first train because it had jumped the rails earlier in the day after a lifetime ambition to drive across roads, grass and sand. There was plenty to observe from my riverside viewpoint, but I diverted my gaze instead to the features on display within the pub I was within.

To my left was an outside stairwell door, and on the wall beside it was an old photograph with the caption: KEW, STRAND ON THE GREEN,

1954. It was black and white, as most historic photos are, and it had a dark border and a lovely golden frame. Savouring the genuine historical nature of its craftsmanship and period features, I began to tightly wring my hands with concern. What if this well-meaning artefact were to be subsequently mass-produced in a Slough factory for some chain pub horror? How could this authentic slice of local past avoid being replicated and dumbed down for some modern, shameless pub hoping to cash in on a heritage of nought?

I assumed my thinking position, placing my face flat on the table surface in the wet condensation that had resulted from my pint glass, and I began racking my brain to think of ways to put the City Barge pub one step ahead of the fake, corporate impostors.

Battlestar Gallactica came to mind immediately, and I decided I'd walk around the bar in a Ceylon suit with a red light pulsing back and forth across my forehead. But Ceylons are actually quite tall and strapping, and given that I would only come up to the waist of the silver metallic suit, causing the crucial top half of the Ceylon to fold over in front and touch its toes, while my nose protruded at waist level like a package of sorts, I began having doubts.

I began having difficulty breathing also, my nostrils quickly becoming water logged, and so I raised my head in a start, heavily snorting condensation in a fountain-like way across the windowpane. Slightly asphyxiated, laughing and weeping, I suddenly hit upon a plan. I would confuse the made-to-order-historical-pub brutes by offering forth a vision of what the view from the City Barge pub may resemble 50 years… into the future. Reaching across, I pulled the historical snapshot of Kew and its hook from the wall and removing the base at the back, I took the slightly faded photograph out of its border and frame. Producing my Finepoint 99-L pen, I began illustrating my outline of 2056.

I started by drawing a few ripples and lines to suggest the river outside was still there, but I proceeded to add huge ships inside large plastic fizzy drink bottles, people in robes walking across the water, and swans that had evolved to look more like dragons. The old greyish-green bridge and noisy trains were nowhere to be seen, a glass skyscraper in the shape of a Phoenix had emerged from the river depths, and the annoying river-view-blocking tree was on fire with roasted pigeons barely clinging to its burnt out, ash-corpse branches. On the opposite bank I added a very slick and towering space shuttle launch pad, and the Strand pathway outside was now a moving escalator carrying pedestrians in shiny clothes with antennas on their heads. Other people were shooting through the air, due to their rocket-shoes, and I also added four suns in the sky, carefully arranging them to resemble a surprised human face. I was adding the finishing touches to the statue of myself when one of the more observant staff members happened to notice the bright, unfaded patch on the wall.

It is often difficult for nice people to accept that there are evil and exploitative forces at work in this world, and allowing for this, I guess the man's apparent anger and outrage were justly channelled as he pointed rudely at the antique photograph now covered in pen scrawl. Smiling like a priest at the funeral of a loved one, I gently began explaining to him how the City Barge was a unique pub, just like he was a unique human being. Character, I opined, is developed over time, and...

The next thing I knew I was being given a fast exit out the door to my left, and as I was escorted down the outdoor staircase, I tried to befriend the well-intentioned barman by spilling out a frenzy of random football results. But I was drowned out by a rather noisy train that was passing over the greyish-green bridge.

Forester

2 Leighton Road W13 9EP
Nearest tube – Northfields

It is often said that a few bars of a song can instantly resurrect deep, well-hidden memories, and now whenever I hear 'The Riddle' by Nick Kershaw, a lump forms in my throat like a ball of wet bread and I'm back at the Forester pub.

The exterior of this fine establishment is almost grand hotel-like in stature, and numerous spacious rooms offer all manner of seating options inside. My half-circular, blue upholstered sofa dominated the area to the left of the central door, and my pint of ale stood resolutely upon a round wooden table with a curious circular wheat motif displayed around its circumference. Bouncing high to test the couch springs, my eyes became drawn to the word BELL that was hand-painted on the support posts at either end of my seat. The post to my left had retained a central white buzzer, housed within a small, round frame, while its opposite had sadly been removed or broken over time.

On the left hand wall was the door to the Gents, and besides this was a cigarette machine, a Lightning 2000 jukebox, and a brightly lit, all-flashing gambling machine. Above these in a glass-fronted presentation box was a stuffed pheasant, and if staring at its round, puffing chest made you hungry, a convenient Thai restaurant was incorporated into the back of the pub, complete with tablecloths, cutlery, napkins, and an automatic cash dispensing machine. Clocking all these details, I then decided to push the white bell on the sturdy wooden supporting post to my left. It compressed with comparative ease, and as it did, a packet of cigarettes dropped with a clunk onto the metal tray of the old brown cigarette machine.

I stared at my shoes for a few minutes before proceeding very slowly towards the machine, coughing loudly to drown out the noise of my rubber soles on the carpet. I retrieved the packet of cigarettes, thinking how they may prove useful in bribing corrupt officials in the Noise Control division of my local council. Back at my seat, I gave the white bell another push, and 'The Riddle' by Nick Kershaw immediately began playing on the Lightning 2000 jukebox. I began a nervous, uncontrollable laughter, but my little snorts were soon drowned out by a cascading flood of coins that tumbled out of the gambling machine in a huge clatter. I had pushed the white bell again.

They were descending in their hundreds, these blimmin' noisy coins, and I noticed the barman walk across to my end of the servery and look at the machine being used by no one. Catching his eye, I held out my arms and pretended to reel in an exceptionally large fish on an imaginary line. Shaking his head, he walked away again.

I have a red hot water bottle for a wallet, and I held it out like a dead chicken, walking with bold strides towards the mountain of coins. I began inserting them into its small circular valve until it was bulging like a rubber porcupine fish. Back at my seat, my face now a similar hue to my wallet, I forced myself to sit quietly and calmly and modestly. Within seconds however, I was furiously jabbing the white bell with my forefinger, growling at it, clouded by a desperate greed for the raw want of more coins. The flashing-light gambling machine remained silent, but a loud pattering noise started to emerge from the rear room that housed the Thai restaurant.

The cash vending machine was vending cash. It was vending wads of cash. Its black dispensing tray was filled to capacity, and small piles of twenty-pound notes had begun to form on the carpet. Removing my grey jersey, I began stuffing the obscene amounts of filthy, dirty cash inside its warm and intimate folds. Back at my blue half-circular couch I sat silently for a time, frowning and thinking that I really should leave. But the white bell was like some kind of Jezebel creature, and I was easily led so I applied a sweaty fingertip to its small ceramic head once more. Nothing happened. A few more jabs, nothing. No sound, no booty.

In some ways I was relieved. I had other pubs to review, places to go. My glass still had a third of ale within, so I quickly downed this and reached for my fattened, sheep-like jersey. And then I heard a noise.

Perplexed, I cautiously looked around, secretly hoping to discover my latest windfall spitting out in a fountain like way. Instead, I looked up to see a most strange sight indeed. A colossal amount of feathers were projecting out at pace from the body of the wall-mounted pheasant. They were softly firing towards the glass walls of its enclosure, creating a 'pak' sound, and causing a scene reminiscent of a pillow fight and a lottery draw.

I stared with opened mouth, unsure how to proceed. How was I to retrieve the feathers without breaking the glass? And where could I possibly store them? Just then, the barman said, "WHAT IN THE LORD'S NAME," and the only complaint I had about the Forester was the taps in the Gents, because you needed to hold them down constantly in order for water to flow, making it very difficult to manage soap and hand washing.

White Cross

Riverside TW9 1TJ
Nearest tube – Richmond tube/rail

The weeping willows on the Richmond riverbank reminded me of candle-wax waterfalls that had congealed mid-cascade, and perhaps one winter evening I will return with some rope and petrol and light them.

Opposite these, a crowd of patrons had gathered outside the White Cross pub, making the most of the fine weather and a lovely view of the Thames. But I chose to head inside the pub instead, scampering up to the impressive Drawing Room where I sat beside a very pretty fireplace with coloured flower tiles.

You'll find no shortage of framed pictures within this large, distinguished room, many of which feature riverside views, or highlight the White Cross pub itself. The green wallpaper behind these is the shade of a sick person's tongue, and its pattern resembles small inkblot tests, in which I saw a sad angel with a head like a stick of corn that had been hung out on a washing line to dry. Of all the pictures in the room, my interest was particularly taken by a black and white illustration of the White Cross that was framed on the wall to my left. Men in small boats featured in the foreground of the picture, along with horses, barrel-laden carts, and a carefully sketched river behind. It was an interesting art piece all told, and I was grateful for the time period parallel between the pub in which I sat and the very same establishment in times long since washed under Richmond Bridge.

A river-facing balcony lead out from the opposite wall, and alongside its iron railings were various seats and tables. An older man in a red chequered shirt sat at one such table with his wife, and my attention was drawn to him via his watch that glistened in the sunlight whenever he moved his hand. His hand would move quite often in fact, because he would wave to every single passing boat on the river. He would wave like mad to them all. I felt embarrassed for him and his wife and for myself, and also for anyone on one of the many passenger boats who happened to witness this humiliating spectacle unfolding. I shook my head sadly, watching him as he rose from his balcony seat, re-entered the Drawing Room, and made his way downstairs via the carpeted stairwell.

Staring absently at the old illustration of the White Cross, thinking back to more sedate and civilised time periods, my eyes suddenly widened at a scene most disturbing. The chequered shirt man who I had just watched descend the staircase had now suddenly appeared in the very drawing before me, and he stood in the illustrated doorway of the White Cross. Although now the size of a 50p coin, he was instantly recognisable in the black and white picture due to his vulgar red top. After navigating his way around a tall woman in a long dress, he marched down the steps, through a picket fence, and across to the river's edge, passing a collection of stray barrels as he went. Upon arrival at the bank's edge, I saw him fumble briefly with his trousers before a stream of his musty yellow urine emerged in a fountain like way to splash into the black and white line-drawing river. The previously rigid old-timers in their carefully crafted boats looked aghast, and one of the nearby horses firmly clomped its hooves in annoyance.

Understandably perturbed myself, I looked across the room to the balcony outside where the disgraced man's wife sat observing the crowd below like an elderly pope on the ledge of the Vatican, sunning herself while a lesser cardinal delivered the prayers. When I turned back to the picture, the culprit was zipping up, and I watched astounded as he began his swagger back towards the front door of the White Cross. A severe defacement of a pleasant scene had occurred in my eyes, and I wasn't about to blend into the sick tongue, sad corn-angel washing line wallpaper and be silent.

When I heard the rogue's brogues stomp back up the carpeted staircase, I moved quickly to meet him at the top, blocking his path with my arms extended on my hips as if to appear larger and wider than I actually was. He paused, bewildered, as I began to shout in clear, considered and earnest tones: "ARE YOU A BEAST? HAVE YOU NOT THE MINUTEST SCRAP OF TASTE AND DECENCY ABOUT YOU?" The man seemed completely astounded and I realised I was spitting slightly. "YOU'RE A BLOODY PISSER!" I screamed. "A BLOODY PISSER!"

A short time afterwards the manager of the White Cross arrived at my table with the man in the red chequered shirt. I pointed to the illustration of the White Cross and re-enacted what I had seen, standing up to add my own visual aids.

As the manager escorted me towards the river's edge, I turned and looked up to the balcony where the wife of the guilty swine was now blessing herself.

White Swan

Riverside TW1 3DN
Nearest tube – Twickenham rail

The White Swan in Twickenham can be reached via a pleasant riverside walk through narrow residential streets, and a sense of quiet calm pervades amidst the soothing sounds of quacking ducks and gentle riverboat engines. I made my approach along a stretch of road known as Riverside, and having just passed a sign that read, ROAD LIABLE TO SUDDEN FLOODING, I noticed with regret that I had wet myself.

Local types nodded in friendly acknowledgement and their well-trained dogs sniffed the air with suspicion as I quickened my pace, hoping to force a breeze upon my damp and tainted crotch. It was a most unusual turn of events that had struck without warning, rendering my lower attire a very real target for ridicule. I attempted to lay the blame with a generous portion of beer glass condensation that I had encountered in the previous public house, or with their new-fangled pushdown taps that had projected water off the porcelain basin like a casually thrown bucket of slops. Whatever the catalyst to my wet trouser patch however, I couldn't escape the perceived reality of the signal I was now emitting, which was one of musty hot urine run amuck.

I decided to conceal the vile spot via a careful realigning of my brown leather satchel, and as I mounted the steep concrete staircase of the White Swan pub, I felt the contents of my bag cascade off each thigh like a series of small sharp waves confronting a rowboat after the wake of a modern, jet-propelled equivalent.

A lovely old timepiece was silent above the bar counter, and dozens of faded nicotine-stained business cards were affixed around the top of the serving area itself. I stared discreetly at the brazen dry crotches around me, admiring their crisp well-pressed form, and after collecting my pint of real ale from the counter, I proceeded at haste towards a wooden bench pew with crimson cushioning that sat to the left of the entrance door. With my lower torso now partially concealed behind a rectangular wooden table, I was able to place my satchel on the bench seat beside me, using my pub review notebook instead to form a roof over my trousers like a black leather sun umbrella.

Looking to my right, I observed some rather embarrassing portrait photographs that were mounted beside the bay conservatory windows. One particular example featured a boy with glasses, ginger hair and a white collar, and there seemed little doubt that his pristine head had at some point been dunked down a grimy school toilet. Laughing, I raised my pint of ale, noticing for the first time a large blue ashtray on my table. It reminded me of a dainty ceramic soap dish, despite the fact that an empty, crinkled up packet of honey-roasted peanuts lay shrivelled and wrinkled within its confines.

As I was replacing my pint of ale upon the table, a solitary bee began hovering around the honey-roasted peanut pack. It was buzzing loudly and it seemed somehow furious. Attempting to swat it away with the back of my hand, I only succeeded in angering it further, and it darted around my face before disappearing somewhere near the portraits in the front bay-window area. Turning back to my glass, I discovered a veritable swarm of bees now buzzing angrily around the crinkled honey-roasted peanut pack in the large blue ashtray. More bees were arriving by the second.

My hands began churning like the blades of a combine harvester in a frantic attempt to shoo away the blighters, but achieving little, I then began swinging my pub review notebook wildly, knocking my pint glass over in the process and dislodging its contents into my lap. Leaping up from my seat as a cloud of bees enfolded me, I stumbled blindly around the bar, my brazen trouser patch now on show for all to see. Ripping down random business cards from above the serving area, I began shouting, "BEEKEEPER! SOMEONE CALL A BEEKEEPER!" No one else in the bar seemed particularly bothered by the bees, and as I ran outside and down the steps, a pack of slobbering dogs began nipping at my heels, chasing me towards the river.

When I emerged from its watery depths soon after, it was not in the manner of a graceful white swan, but more in the style of a cigarette end that has resurfaced amidst the unfinished dregs in a pint of murky beer.

Acknowledgements

London Pub Reviews has been independently published, but only with the support and encouragement of many people.

Very special thanks to Laura, John, Mark, Jon, Martin and to all my extended family.

A huge thanks to DWE Rhodes for his unswerving help and advice.

Thanks also to Roger Kennedy, Mejor Singh, David Le Fleming, Steve MacDonald, Andrew Stevens, Heidi James at Social Disease, Matthew Coleman, Emily Moore at Tank Magazine, Kriston Ware, Tom McCarthy, Steven Hall, Pablo Videla, Joel & Ila de Mello Bradley, James Kieron Taylor, Trefor & Mel Thomas, Jessamy Robinson, Dan Cole, Howard Green, Ian Owen, Brian Robinson, Ed Robinson, Dave Askwith, Eoghain Clarke and Phil Clarke.

Special thanks to Yves and Teo.

To CAMRA for their dedication to the preservation of the London pub, and for their continued support of the small brewery.

To all the publicans of the pubs within this book, thank you for your warm hospitality, and for the ready supply of soap within your bathrooms.

A number of these stories first appeared in other places. Thanks to Toby Litt, Ali Smith and the British Council for inclusion in New Writing 13 (Sun Tavern, Covent Garden; Prince of Wales, Covent Garden); thanks to Andrew Gallix at 3:AM (Champion, Fitzrovia; Prince George, Hackney; Surprise in Chelsea, Chelsea), and to James Bridle at Snow Books who reproduced the 3:AM stories in The Edgier Waters: Five Years of 3:AM (edited by Andrew Stevens); to Lee Rourke at Scarecrow (French House, Soho); to Vim Cortez at Paris Bitter Hearts Pit (Albert, Victoria), and to Steve Farrar at the Times Higher Education Supplement for commissioning the Jeremy Bentham, Bloomsbury.

And to my wife Linda, for the many late night police station visits, the flowers at the hospitals, the bail money, the legal representation, and for the many laughs and much love and happiness. Thank you.

Thank you for visiting: www.londonpubreviews.co.uk